STANDS WITH FISTS

MOVING BEYOND PSYCHOLOGICAL AND VERBAL ABUSE

A TRUE STORY AND
PROFESSIONAL GUIDE
TO HEALING

DEBBIE ZOUB, MSW

╫**RICHER Press**
An Imprint of Richer Life, LLC

RICHER Press is a full service, specialty Trade publisher whose sole goal is to *shape thoughts and change lives for the better*. All of the books, eBooks and digital media we publish, distribute and market embrace our commitment to help maximize opportunities for personal growth and professional achievement.

To learn more visit
www.richerlifellc.com.

Copyright © 2013 by Debbie Zoub

Published by ╫RICHER Press
An Imprint of Richer Life, LLC

4600 E. Washington Street, Suite 300, Phoenix, Arizona 85034
www.richerlifellc.com

Cover Design: Richer Media USA • Photographs: Sharon Martin and Big Stock Photo

Library of Congress Cataloging-in-Publications Data

Stands With Fist
Moving Beyond Psychological and Verbal Abuse
Debbie Zoub, MSW -- 1ˢᵗ edition
p.   cm.

1. Self-Help 2. Educational 3. Abuse
ISBN 978-0-9899001-1-9
 (pbk : alk. Paper)

2013951953

ISBN 13: 978-0-9899001-1-9

ISBN 10: 0-9899001-1-9

Text set is Adobe Garamond

PRINTED IN THE UNITED STATES OF AMERICA

First edition
December 2013

DEDICATION

Debbie Zoub 1964

I dedicate this book to my inner little girl and the young children inside every person who has endured abuse. I am still amazed by my child's ability to survive the scary reality that was forced upon her at such a young, tender age. Her tenacity, grit, and determination to keep walking forward have been my blessing and gift, for it is she who kept us alive. While she can still exhaust me, I will spend the rest of my life hugging and nurturing her as we heal and move forward.

She has been my rock, and now it's my turn to be hers.

*"And the day came
when the risk it took
to remain tight in the bud
was more painful
than the risk it took
to blossom."*

~ Anaïs Nin ~

TABLE OF CONTENTS

TABLE OF CONTENTS

ACKNOWLEDGEMENTS

It is with all my heart and spirit that I'd like to thank my loving, wonderful support system that took this journey of healing and recovery with me. Each one of you held a special place that allowed me to verbalize, struggle, and vent as you listened and helped me move forward. Your guidance and encouragement got me to a place where I finally understood my reality and I was able to let go of what was, a place I could not have reached alone. It really does take a village.

MY MOTHER

I know some will feel I betrayed you by writing this. Most have given me loving support and words of empowerment as I walked through the journey that is this book. I am certain of how proud you are of my resolve to help make a difference for others living a life of pain and abuse, because that is what you were all about: making a difference in people's lives. If this book does what I believe it will, many will leave their abusive situations and move toward lives of purpose, health, prosperity, and peace. My hope is that your death will save many lives. No matter what anyone thinks, I know you are looking down and are proud because secrets don't matter to you anymore.

STACEY KRAMER - EDITOR

I want to thank my editor and friend, Stacey Kramer. You did an incredible job of learning my story, getting to know me, and helping me organize my thoughts and writing. You made this book flow with your brilliance. I can feel your heart in every word and chapter.

JUDI LEE GOSHEN

You have known me since the beginning and our tie is long. You have watched and listened. We carry each other's stories and know them well. In beginning this journey, I had to hear my own voice, not the voice of even my closest friends. I was unable to decipher all the advice. I had to grow up, had to guide myself through these life decisions. Thank you for teaching me that, in the process of attaining freedom, you may lose good people along with the bad—but the best will always take you back. I am grateful for our friendship and sisterhood. I love you, always and forever.

SUZY ULMER

You are one of two people in my life who has always had my back and never judged me. While others may question our connection, we never have.

SOPHIA ULMER

The little girl I have known since birth to the beautiful woman you are today, my dear Sophalicious. Your ability to hear my story and read my words without touching my voice helped me complete this book. With your own history of adult abusive relationships, we were able to come together with a lot of laughter and tears as we made soft and loud music in our collaboration. What a team we have made. The magic of your love, tenacity, grit, and determination as my second editor helped give birth to this book.

DIANE MOORE

Words fail me when I try to express what you have meant to me. It has been with your guidance, patience, compassion, and caring that I was able to make my journey towards peace and freedom a reality. You are a true spirit and gift who was placed in my path of healing.

BARNEY

In your quest for anonymity, I will not use your name. You will forever be known to many as my dear friend Barney. I thank you for our friendship. It has taught me the purity of two people wanting each other to succeed and be happy. You have been a tower of strength for me always, even in my darkest moments. You are a blessing.

PAULA SALKY

Thank you for your friendship and creative guidance in helping me perceive the book cover. Your vision was brilliant.

LINDA RANDALL, MY SECOND GRADE SCHOOL TEACHER

Thank you for the morning in class, a particularly bad day for me, when you called me up to stand beside you as you read a book. You did not know it was a bad day for me, yet you lovingly stroked my hair as you read. You made me feel counted and seen that morning in my invisible world, a moment I still remember clearly.

SHARON MARTIN

Our friendship will always mean the world to me. My sadness at its demise and my sole participation in that reality will hurt forever. Thank you for slowly taking me back in the fold and accepting my apology.

JUDGE EDDIE

Thank you for your lifetime of kindness, fatherly love, compassion, and caring. You will have a place in my heart forever.

DEBBIE TAITEL

Thank you for your friendship and walking through this with me.

DAN FOLEY

Having you in my corner through the journey that became this book has been a gift and a blessing. Thanks for standing by me, always.

JASON LACY

Thank you for your kindness, standing by my side and gentle guidance through this process. You helped make a difficult journey possible. Like Dan, it has been a gift to have you in my corner.

RICHER PRESS

Thanks to Earl Cobb, Richer life, LLC and the entire RICHER Press team for refining my manuscript and doing an exceptional job in publishing this book. The entire experience was both enjoyable and rewarding.

SPECIAL ACKNOWLEDGEMENTS go to HARRIET FREIBERGER, WANDA ELY, and the ART DEPOT WRITER'S GROUP, as well as to DR. DAVID CRISTE and ANDREA HYAMS, who literally put my body back together, to JILL MURPHY LONG, who helped me begin the journey of this book, and to MARILYN VAN DERBUR, who taught me how to stand tall.

And finally, to BO, my cute, funny, smart, engaging dog. Bo showed me what unconditional love is all about. Since my mother's death, he has stuck by my side with his funny face, abundant amounts of love, and wet kisses. He's been there to walk "one step at a time" with me.

FORWARD
By Sophia Ulmer

To the readers of this book, so full of promise:

Abuse is powerful: so powerful, in fact, it often holds us more tightly than love. We may even mistake it for love, which is—after all—its favorite mask. Perhaps the most devastating of abuse's attributes is this deceptive ability. Further exacerbating this situation is that these most vile expressions of human emotion are so often confused with the purest—with love— which I like to imagine as a glistening glass of transparent water. Abuse, on the other hand, is motor oil—an ever-thickening black toxicity. One drop in the water glass may produce a seductive iridescence, dangerous and energetic like a puddle of gasoline. Another drop, heavy, may pool at the bottom, joining with the first like mercury, strengthening. The water may be fine to drink, though not as quenching as before. The flavor change may be undetectable yet. How puzzling, we may think, to get heartburn from something rumored to be *life-giving*.

Drip, drip, drip.

When shaken, the two substances begin to seem interchangeable, one in the same, a love slickened with grease then studded with grit. Drip, drip, drip. Eventually, the oil will rise to the top and stay there. The purity is gone. Drink up.

Debbie and my mother have been friends since college. I was the first baby born into this social group, and have fond memories of spending time with Debbie when I was young,

13

idolizing her cascading hair, inspecting her collection of dangly beaded earrings as if they were artifacts in a museum. I've always been intrigued by her, the maid of honor in my parents' wedding—drawn to her unabashed goofiness, her fierce intelligence, her purposeful gait. Though she has been around since the beginning of my life, we were separated by generations, and I knew very little of Debbie's family or personal life. Though she lovingly admonishes her defensive shell, Debbie is the woman who, when I went to college, taught me how to be tough—big-city tough. *You own this city. Pretend you've lived here your entire life. No one fucks with you—got it?* In this way, even before the experience of working with her on this book, she gave me fists, which kept me safe.

I met her mother once, when I was in college, at an art show. She flitted around like a hummingbird—if a hummingbird wore massive, stylish glasses. She was certainly high-strung, but undeniably magnetic, the embodiment of cosmopolitan: glamorous, intellectual. Though I was at least a head taller, I felt microscopic in her presence. This feeling was most certainly intensified by that fact that I was simultaneously suffering in my engagement to a psychologically abusive man. (The physical and sexual abuse in this relationship was fortunately mild—albeit dysfunctional and unhealthy—but nonetheless prevalent and painful.) The difference between my situation and Debbie's is that she was born into her abuse. I have felt that I *chose* mine. So what would spur a young woman from a loving family to enter relationships with abusive men? This has, after all, been going on since high school, when my first boyfriend—though he has since grown into a genuine friend—would scream himself red-eyed and hoarse in jealous fits. Why did I do this to myself? What is *wrong with me?*

These people, in the beginning at least, smell fresh, taste sweet, whisper all the right things. And suppose they come into our lives in a time when we are naïve (and we all have been before), or heartbroken, wandering or wondering or otherwise uncertain. The first attacks come suddenly, in an argument. The violence escalates in its vocabulary, or in a physical assault. And then the aftermath: They are perhaps as shocked as we are. They vow to never again. And the second time, the same. But they still smell good. They still taste the same as they did in the beginning, so we trick ourselves once. Just once. Three strikes, we think. So when they kiss us now, we hesitate, though secretly relish their attention, their affection. We keep faith.

The third time: is it. And they cry. And they beg. And we feel. We feel for them because of the way their elbows crease, because of the wrinkles around their eyes when they smile. We fall more deeply for our memories, for the weekend getaways of any newly minted pairing, still applying gloss to itself, oblivious. We perhaps love their families by now, or their pets, or we perhaps have accumulated pets with them, grown our own branches, fashioned nests. But sometimes it's inexplicable, how incredibly unreliable we can be to ourselves.

We all perhaps know, deep down, why we stay. Perhaps these people are familiar: Our distinction between love and abuse has always been warbling in and out of focus. Or we could be sensitive, or maybe just lonely. Surely we trick ourselves into fearing loneliness more than we fear abuse. And besides, these attacks usually have reprieves rendered ethereal in their contrast. Even the most voracious waves recede with the tide, but abuse is tying our wrists, anchoring our ankles. *Loneliness will drown you forever*, is its constant threat. *You are a monster if you leave. You made a promise.* And, although we each carry exactly enough power to control our own paths through this life, we may have convinced ourselves otherwise. We may be lost, the biggest source of tragedy. We have been caught in a cyclone—which way is up? In my case, it was the general malaise of youth—the poor self-

15

esteem and insecurity and sensitivity—combined with a passion for helping people. My good-natured intents went awry, my capacity to forgive too great. I had no boundaries. I thought I'd found love. My fiancé was a mastermind of manipulation, a military man—cutting you down to build you back up.

Like Debbie, I was always trying to stay ahead of the abuse. I began habitually lying to my abuser to prevent confrontation, even when there was nothing to be confronted about. I just *knew* he'd find a way. When I was in school and spent time apart, he would ignore my calls at night—he later told me of his infidelities. Often when we would talk, an argument would ensue, and he would begin to shout, or hiss. He would twist my tongue as I dissociated. He taunted me, called me names like *crazy bitch*, *cunt*, and—perhaps his personal favorite—*dumb-dumb*, and was dismissive and unsupportive of my education and art, belittling my ambitions as petty. He humiliated me, both privately and in front of his friends, then trap me with an excuse, a reason why I'd hurt him, why I'd deserved it. How he was real sorry, but...

There was always a reprieve, and I lived for them. He was a musician, you see, and I just loved how he'd sing to me, how he substituted my name into "Wagon Wheel." He was also very intelligent, and in the beginning I enjoyed our challenging conversations. (The sex, I realize as I've gotten older, was mediocre.) He would sometimes apologize, but usually I'd let him get off consequence-free. Since he was working and I was in school, he would buy me lavish gifts then remind me incessantly of their value and his sacrifice. He had every reason to be misogynistic or racist, and to laugh at me when I'd protest. He was too smart to think that way, and how could I think he was serious? He had every right to blast hateful music, despite my requests—then pleas—to turn it down, my eardrums wailing in pain. I was told where to go, what I should do, say, wear, and

16

who I could talk to. He would go through my phone and read my journal, using jealousy to justify his baseless suspicions. Until the final two weeks of our three-year relationship, I was as faithful as a rug—powerless, brainwashed, fearful, shameful. Abused.

Debbie writes of being "in the hole," the dark abyss we seem to occupy during these times, or when we are abusing ourselves. In my hole, I felt like my abusers were colonizing my body and mind, slowing taking me over as their own. I grind my teeth ferociously at night, much like Debbie would clench her fists. During my abusive relationship, I developed bulimia—I believe at first to locate *something* I could control—and other addictive patterns followed. I dissociated frequently and was depressed constantly. But I had friends and family who supported me with honesty, so I never yearned for dreamlessness.

I still have trouble. I anticipate and fear that unrealistic expectations will be put upon me by a romantic partner. I am sensitive by nature, and my abuse has made me hyper-conscious of the spoken tone. I value my aversion to fighting, but acknowledge that I often fly—leaving destruction behind. I still struggle with body image and boundaries, with trusting good and not overreacting to bad. Today, I'm taking care of myself. My journey began four years ago, when I left my abusive situation. I've recovered from my eating disorder and have found solace in friendships, some therapy, and—for difficult times—a low doses of anti-depressants. I do my yoga, I read, I write. I am free to write what I want, and find joy in creating poetic beauty, even if its catalyst was an experience of pain. I love food and cooking, travel, film, tutoring, swimming in the ocean, and engaging with people at work and school. Most importantly, I surround myself with people who love me.

Having lunch with a wise friend recently, in the south on the Atlantic coast—perhaps my equivalent to Debbie's mountains—he used the term *co-independence*. Co-independence is what exists in any healthy, functioning relationship. The participants in the relationship or family dynamic support one another with kindness and guidance, yet operate independently, always respecting the diversity of personality, opinion, and lifestyle. How would wider usage of this word change the way we enter and interact in relationships? The simultaneously heartening and devastating fact is that psychological abuse permeates so many relationships. Even if we ourselves have not been abused, we all know abused people. We know abusers, as well—though, they have usually been abused as well. This awareness brings a broader idea of sympathy into focus: sympathy for the unknown. If you have never been abused, how do you help? We enter the world with openness and grace, knowing that we cannot offer ourselves to others until we first care for ourselves. We realize that the only stipulation of intelligence is the consistent desire to learn. You embrace the fundamental truth that we *choose* to be lonely, that there are always those out there who know, in fact, how to love.

PREFACE

I TELL THIS STORY TO YOU WITHOUT VIOLINS in the background; I am not interested in sympathy. I tell it with no drama or movie-of-the-week sentimentality. It was what it was and **it is what it is**. I tell this story because it is time to move beyond abuse. I validate your experience and I am here to say that it is true, it happened, and it is real. You cannot fix it or change it, but you *can* do something for yourself. It is time for you to **let yourself off the hook**. I say this with compassion and a knowing reality: Let it go. The journey is not easy—and at times debilitating, overwhelming, and messy,—but, with time, you can be free.

In the appendix, which is comprised of the **bolded terms**, I give you a language for the diagnostic fallout from abuse as well as for the recovery process. It is my belief that we have lived our lives reacting to abuse and that our symptoms are not disorders. This is my way of **normalizing the abnormal**. There are many psychotherapeutic diagnoses given to those who are being or were abused and seek professional help, such as **post-traumatic stress**, anxiety, **depression reaction, dissociative reaction,** and **obsessive reaction**. You may be experiencing some or all of the effects listed in the appendix due to your circumstances. These reactions and coping mechanisms have kept you alive and helped guide you through your survival. These are brilliant responses to dealing with that which is so out of control. I have taken these professional clinical disorders and put them into a language all can understand.

19

My intention is not to diagnose anyone with any type of psychological disorder or medical condition, but to give you a vocabulary for and understanding of what you may be feeling. Having a language to describe what you are going through is powerful. There is brilliance in understanding and using these emotional realities so you can begin to find your tools for the recovery process. Simply consider how the terms may fit your situation as a way to start defining for yourself what is happening, or happened. You might even have some to add that are not listed and fit your own personal experience. Know that if any of the criteria listed fits, you are not crazy. The information is only to normalize your abnormal experience. These reactions have served to help you function within the dysfunction that is, or was, your life. You are not sick; you are surviving.

Also in the Appendix, I define the terms I have worked with throughout my own life. These are expressions I have either come up with or heard others say and used to help me understand my reality. These sayings are used throughout the book. They are my mantras, so to speak, in the moments I need them. This renaming has been my way of taking the power of clinical diagnoses and reclaiming their meaning for myself.

Let me state here that I am not a doctor, and if you are experiencing somatic (physical), physiological (interfering with normal healthy physical functioning) and/or psychological (emotional, spiritual, mental) symptoms, *they are real.* You should always address these symptoms by seeking appropriate medical and psychological intervention. The appendix is simply devoted to helping you make sense of how minds and bodies may respond to abuse and give you a language for understanding what may be happening. What you are feeling cannot be disputed. They are your feelings and your experiences. Remember, it is these feelings that are warning you to do something about your situation. I say that because we are all survivors, and you are much stronger than you think. Once you know better, you do better. Now it is time to learn and do something different and healthier.

Finally, I did not write this book with the intent of hurting or bashing. This is not written in an accusatory manner, nor is it intended to denigrate anyone. I am not writing a "Mommy Dearest," and I have no interest in the blame game. I loved my abusers in spite of everything; it's what made it so difficult to leave. I have let go and am still learning. Most days I've moved on and away, and I want to help others living in or recovering from abuse to find their own voices and power, to stop feeling invisible. This is a book about educating, healing, and taking responsibility for yourself, and, if you have them, your children. It is to validate the experiences of those living in abuse and provide tools to understand, deal with, and journey towards health and freedom. This is my story of living a life in the most confusing and frustrating manner, then rejecting the behaviors of my abusers in order to take responsibility for my healing and recovery. Abuse is about the journey out. It is part of the healing process and keeping one out of harm's way. It is the journey I am still on. In my struggle, I have realized you can't always get what you want. So I am moving towards getting what I need: a voice and to help others find theirs. It is also for professionals who work with the abused to help them better understand what we are going through.

I haven't forgiven the abuse. I believe there is nothing to forgive. What I *have* forgiven is my inability to stop it, or protect myself from it as a child and into adulthood. I have given up the hope that my past could have been any different and have stopped trying to rewrite it. My anger is gone, at least most days. Yet, there are times when the exhaustion still exists and I take many steps backwards. Broken bones heal; bruises heal. The invisible breaks to the heart and spirit also cause damage. You can do something about the pain. The memories can soften, just as scars fade. You never forget, yet freedom is attainable. The work of recovery is hard, but it is honest.

Let's take this journey together.

NOTE TO MY READERS:

This book is written to share with you both my *memories* and *feelings* as well as my *professional and clinical prospective.*

Please note that the "text" associated with my professional clinical prospective IS shaded...similar to this box.

The "text" associated the memories and feelings IS NOT shaded.

PROLOGUE

*It has been said, "Time heals all wounds." I do not agree.
The wounds remain.*

*In time, the mind, protecting its sanity, covers them with
scar tissue and the pain lessens. But it is never gone.*

~ Rose Kennedy ~

GOODBYE MOM

On a sunny June day, my mother was killed by her partner
of twenty-three years. I will refer to him as Jack. I have to
believe—need to believe—that this was a tragedy, a horrific
accident waiting to happen. Not murder. But it doesn't matter,
because the outcome is the same. My mother died at the hands of
a miserable man who brought her along for the ride. And still she
wouldn't leave; my mother stayed, stayed until she was dead.

Jack was the man I grew to call stepfather, though he and
my mother never married. I was close to him, as my relationship
with my own father was a struggle—when it existed at all. Jack
could be very kind, but was also emotionally cruel. So filled with
rage, he was a man who could kill with words. I participated in
the cycle of abuse he and my mother called a relationship by
keeping it a secret. I will never know what he was thinking when
he ran her over with a golf cart, crushing her tiny body. He

23

wouldn't talk, and took any answers with him when he died a year and a half later.

My mother was a very strong woman, yet she chose psychologically abusive men who allowed her spirit to be beaten down, men who didn't know how to love. My father emotionally crushed her, then abandoned her and their children, projecting blame on everyone but himself. Most people knew that about my father, but what they didn't know was that Jack was verbally and emotionally abusive as well. That fact she kept secret for years from all but a few select friends who didn't really know the extent of the abuse. But I did: I watched and heard it all, and, in the last two years of her life, knew he was going to kill her. Intuition told me so.

Towards the end, I pleaded with her to finally speak to her friends and neighbors about the danger in which she was living. I begged and begged as her anxiety grew, but she was too embarrassed to let the outside in. After her death, I was heartbroken that she was too beaten down to ask for help, though also bitter that she had dumped all her rage, anxiety, and fears on me. I could not have helped by sharing the details of her inner world without betraying her trust. But that's how it works, doesn't it? You have to keep the secrets at all costs. You feel you must; fear and embarrassment overwhelm the abused. It is a heavy emotional burden for a daughter who intellectually and professionally knows there was nothing I could have done to save my mother, because even as a clinical social worker who understands the dynamics of psychological abuse, I felt unable to stop the insanity. I could not make a large enough impact to change her life. I was in a paralyzing cycle, with an inability to scream out and bring in help. It would have devastated my mother. It would have blown her front. It would have stopped the abuse.

24

It would have stopped the abuse!

I had to come to a realization that I was unable to create change, unable to save my mother, yet unable to walk away. I was powerless. And now she is dead and I wonder: the secrets, all those secrets in a lifetime of abuse, would telling have changed anything? This is what is in my head, the head of a competent, smart woman and adult child of abuse. Keeping the secrets of verbal and emotional abuse, and for what? Was it to protect the raging, angry man? To protect my mother from being devastated by humiliation and shame? Keeping the secrets killed her.

Since beginning this book, I woke up each morning—or in the middle of the night—and thought about what I wanted to write and how to write about it. My home décor took on a yellow sticky note motif. They were everywhere. I have so many memories; my experience is vast and multi-faceted. It is with this knowledge I want to talk about why people stay in abusive relationships. It is clear we don't have to live this way, so why is it so difficult to leave? What keeps us stuck? For me, the difficulty was the fiercely protective stance I took with my mother—no matter how she treated me. She was an amazing person and I loved her very much; it was a real cycle of love and hate. She was fearful, ashamed, and lost in her world of abuse.

Toward the end of her life, she began to talk about leaving Jack, but felt people would think she was a horrible person for abandoning him as his health deteriorated. She did not let anyone know how bad things were, particularly that his anger and rage were escalating. She hid this from the outside world. To most people, Jack was this kind and gentle giant. She forbade me from discussing his abusive side with others, creating a secret world of abuse within the confines of her home. She was embarrassed, she was anxious, and she was scared. She was stuck. So was I.

How can one understand cruelty? How does one understand abuse when healing is impossible unless you leave? The chances of it changing, after all, tend to be slim. So I am left with the remnants of that complicated relationship called mother and daughter. She loved and adored me the only way she knew how. The comfort in discomfort of abuse was our connection, but in a heartbeat, all I had known and lived came to an end.

With the tragedy of my mother's death comes my time to get the conversation started on a new level, to shake things up and help those living in or recovering from abuse move away from the shame and secrets. It is time for abusers to assume responsibility for their behavior and for us to hold them accountable. My wish is to up the ante on how we deal with and understand psychological abuse because our society still does not view it in the same realm as physical and sexual abuse. It is hard to come up with statistics on verbal and emotional abuse. I believe it is under reported. For the purpose of this book, I'm not going to try. Just know that it is real.

How do we make it safe for the abused to tell their stories and get out? How do we reach abusers, talk to the monster? How can we access that dark place so well insulated by the participants? The answer for those being abused seems easy. You just leave. But if it were so easy, wouldn't my mother have just left? Wouldn't I have told her secrets? Wouldn't I have walked away from my own abuse long ago? For such an easy answer, why is the reality of leaving impossible for so many? And so this book was born.

I start the conversation with my personal story, my knowledge and the care and compassion that I extend to all of you through the lessons I've learned and am still learning. Having been a clinical social worker for more than two decades, I have worked with all types of abuse and neglect, as well as with survivors of sexual abuse as young as five years old. I've even worked with sexual perpetrators both adult and adolescent. I will share both my professional knowledge and personal life events to connect with those living in abuse. Through my words, my hope is that you will find your own voice.

This has been a lifetime coming. It is something I have wanted to do forever: write about the impact of all **abuses**, with the main focus being **psychological abuse**. Growing up in abuse made that so, and with my mother's death, I can now do this. My name is Debbie, but my Native American name should be **Stands with Fists**. Not in violence, but because I am the resilient child who spent a lifetime in a stance of grit and determination, ready to ward off all the evil around me. I always stood ready to fight, protecting myself from the unpredictable world in which I was trying to survive. Sad, yes, but it helped me to become a **survivor** of abuse. My message is clear: Abuse, in all forms, is **unacceptable**.

Abusive relationships are destructive and exasperating. They are lose/lose situations, always. Abusers sling damaging attacks—whether verbal, emotional, sexual, or physical—with no regard towards those they assault. Psychological attacks are always difficult because the blows are invisible. Abuse is abuse no matter what methods are exhibited. If you are neglected or abused physically, sexually, and/or psychologically (an umbrella term I will use for verbal/emotional), it is all abuse. The scars are the same, only the broken bones, violations, and bruises are invisible in neglect, verbal, and emotional abuse. Yet, it is no less damaging to the heart and soul.

My understanding about my fists began in my thirties as I was lying in bed with a boyfriend. He took my right hand and began massaging it. He told me I would clench my fists into tight little balls and that is how I fell asleep, every night. I did not know this, had never noticed. That night, I cried **invisible tears,** still unable to cry out loud, embarrassed by any show of sadness and vulnerability to the outside world. After that, I looked for pictures of me as a child. I could not find many, but the ones I did find showed a scrawny little kid with unkempt hair and a defiant facial expression standing with her tightly clenched fists, the fists I apparently had not given up since childhood. My fists were a statement of a very frightened little girl. I carried them everywhere with me. After that night, when I would go to bed, I consciously unclenched and massaged my own hands. I learned how to relax them, both in bed and out in the world. It took a while.

What is Abuse?

How is abuse defined? What are its shapes and forms, and what does it do to the human spirit? What are the lifetime patterns abuse sets up for young children, and what is the fallout once they reach adulthood? From all I have studied and read, I have not been able to find a universally accepted definition of verbal and emotional abuse. Experts do agree it is a pattern of behavior. This lack of clarity only escalates the danger the abused feel. This is unacceptable, as the lack of outward signs makes legal intervention against an abuser very difficult. In many cases, legal action intensifies the abuse, and without the same protections as for the sexually and physically abused. It becomes he-said-she-said.

I will convey what I know professionally and personally about psychological abuse. Each definition depends on personal experience, so put your own reality in place of mine when our experiences differ. I want my story to resonate, so you will feel I am speaking directly to you. This book is about our commonality. We have been deeply affected by this and it has touched every aspect of our lives. This is how we have lived with, concealed, and hidden out behind the abuse. I give you a road map, so make it your own. Begin to define your needs and wants so you can begin, or continue, your journey to freedom.

I am going to focus on psychological abuse, the weapons of which are unseen. It is my belief that emotional and verbal abuses, due to their invisible nature, are the least understood and need to have their own voice. Having been the main form of abuse I have experienced throughout my life (as well as some physical and sexual abuse), part of my difficulty being able to leave was due to the my own lack of understanding, as well as having my voice minimized by others when I *did* attempt to tell. I believe my abusive reality was never given the validity it deserved.

To me, verbal and emotional abuse is a deliberate pattern of behavior on the part of the abuser that is always about power and control over those they abuse. I have always felt that abusers abuse because they don't feel good or secure about themselves. They have a damaged sense of self-worth and very poor-esteem. By pulling the person they abuse down with them, it provides the abuser a sense of superiority. They need those around them to feel worse than they do about themselves to feel powerful and in control. If the abuser can make you believe that you are **less-than**, they feel powerful. The way that behavior is inflicted causes serious interference in the growth potential of the person on the receiving end. Due to never feeling safe or emotionally secure in abuse, self-esteem is destroyed. Our senses of self diminish until we feel worthless and many of us will begin to abuse ourselves by believing the abuser. Verbal and emotional abuse often increases in intensity as it goes on and can lead to physical abuse. This is a nice neat explanation for what makes an abuser abuse. The reality of living in this is a lot more complicated.

Verbal and emotional abuse can happen in any area of life. It can happen to anyone regardless of educational level, economic

29

background, gender, race, culture, religion, or age. Case in point: I am Jewish, white, and well-educated. I was raised by a single mother who built a very successful business with very little money. I am well-traveled and have been able to experience many fine things. My background did not stop the abuse from happening, nor prevent the effects it has had on my life. It does not matter who you are or where you come from, abuse happens and abuse is abuse.

Maybe you were not born into abuse. You may have first experienced it as an adult. Perhaps you met a charming, smart, seductive person who gave you a sense of wellbeing. This person was loving, kind, compassionate, and made you feel safe. You were drawn in, hooked. You felt you had found "the one," and you fell in love. Slowly, it began to shift. Little things crept in. When you think about it, you are not sure where or when these changes occurred. An explosive one-time rage out of nowhere may have been followed with flowers, or a dinner out with the promise it would never happen again. The shelf-life of these promises, however, became shorter and shorter—then they maybe disappeared completely. Before you knew it, your violent situation had escalated, and not only are you unable to process its insanity, you do not have a clue how to respond. Perhaps when the abuse occurs, you convince yourself it will never happen again. While you know it probably will, you wish, you pray, you hope, you so want to believe this is the last of these episodes, which have become as commonplace as the good times. You slowly become the *cause* of the abusive behavior. "If you hadn't done this, I wouldn't have had to do that." You begin to blame yourself, indoctrinated by the worthlessness being instilled in your psyche. Maybe you are still trying to fix it, making yourself believe that you can get that person you first met back. Your life becomes living in between the episodes. With so many forms and packages in which abuse is perpetrated, our commonality is the feeling that we are walking on very thin ice, desperate not to step too heavily.

Some of you are still surviving abuse. Some have found your way out and are on the journey to heal the invisible wounds and quiet your heart. Since there are no visible bruises or broken bones with psychological abuse, it can make our realities difficult to understand, not only for outsiders, but to ourselves as well. No matter how or when it began, please know you are not alone. Please know psychological violence can at any time become physical, and loving your abuser comes with a high personal price tag. And even though I believe Jack didn't intend to kill my mother, she is dead.

I am going to give you a reality check on what verbal and emotional abuse looks, sounds, and feels like in the hopes of validating your experience. I want to provide concrete examples of normal vs. extreme behavior in relationships. Take your time with these lists as you figure out which descriptions fit your experience. Those being abused with cruel words, whether orally or in written form, deserve a voice and better diagnostic criteria. It is getting better, but more work needs to be done. It needs to be dealt with as what it is: abuse. Those experiencing and living with it should know it exists and is real. If you are in a situation where the verbal and emotional cruelty is killing your spirit or the spirits of your children, even if it is invisible, you are being abused. You and your **family** are suffering. If you can relate to any of what I say, if it describes your experience, know that you are not the problem and you are not crazy. You are being abused.

QUESTIONS TO ASK YOURSELF

- Are you consumed by the relationship, thinking *What now? What next?*
- Are you always trying to stay ahead of the abuse?
- Are you ignored, disrespected, and criticized?
- Berated, lied to, taunted, and put down?
- Do you feel powerless, brainwashed, or crazy?
- Do phrases like these sound familiar?
  - *Stupid bitch.*
  - *Worthless.*
  - *Whore.*
  - *Cunt.*
  - *It's all your fault.*
  - *You are nothing without me.*
  - (Etcetera, etcetera, etcetera…)
- Do you feel trapped by humiliation and threats?
- Are you made to feel ashamed or embarrassed, whether privately or in front of others?
- Do you feel as though the expectations put upon you are unreasonable?
- Do you feel as though you are held to an impossible standard?
- Do you submit to undesired behavior in order to avoid conflict?
- Is sexual contact ever forced upon you?
- Are you told whom you may talk to?
- What you can say, do, go, or wear?
- Do you feel your personal **boundaries** and need for privacy are respected?
- Have any of your personal belongings been destroyed?

- Do you feel paralyzed by fear and shame?
- Are you resistant to change?
- Does the abuse escalate if you stand up for yourself?
- Are you financially dependent on your abuser(s)?
- Do your family members and friends receive undue criticism with the intent of causing your estrangement from them?
- Are you prevented from seeing family and friends or stopped seeing them on your own due to embarrassment and shame?
- Have you been accused of being abusive?
- Do you feel sick and tired of being sick and tired, and then become exhausted by being so sick and tired of being sick and tired?

QUESTIONS TO ASK YOURSELF ABOUT YOUR ABUSER(S)

- Do they[1] let you know you are a failure?
- Do they place blame on others, calling them idiots or stupid?
- Do they stalk or harass you, either physically or technologically?
- Do they question everything you do?
- Are they allowed to behave in any manner they choose without consequence?
- Do they threaten to kill themselves, you, the children, or the pets if you leave?
- Do they try to make you believe no one else would want you?
- Do they manipulate your words to confuse you?

---

[1] "They" is used to maintain gender neutrality, regardless of whether or not you have one or more abuser(s) in your life.

- Do they intimidate you through looks or gestures?
- Do they ever threaten to use weapons?
- Do they control your computer time or what you read and watch on television?
- Do they check your phone or screen your calls?
- Do they use jealousy to justify their actions or reactions?
- Do they deny that they are abusing you?
- After an episode, is there calm after the storm?
- Do they threaten to expose your secrets such as sexual orientation or immigration status? (As an example of immigration threat, I had a Latino client. Her husband came to this country and gained legal immigration status. He learned to speak English when he got here. He brought his wife, my client, over, but did not legalize her. Her ability to speak English was limited. They had children who are legal U.S. citizens. Her husband abused her and then threaten if she told, he would have her deported and she would never see her children again.)

Are these types of behavior really *abuse*? My answer is a resounding *yes*: Psychological abuse is real. The difference is there may be no physical violence, but the internal pain and scarring is valid. When you live a **life** dictated by this type of abuse, when you actually start believing what your abuser is telling you, you are in trouble. Living your life feeling stupid, worthless, and invisible is merely a reaction to a life lived in survival mode. Because remember, abuse is never your fault.

Once I learned what abuse was, I began to understand its meaning and affects as well as *why* some people abuse others. I had to keep reminding myself that the abuse was about the people who abuse, not about me. This was especially important when in the midst of an attack. At first, this was hard to

34

remember, because lifelong habits are difficult to break—and being abused *always* hurts. However, it was now up to me how I deal with the pain.

I am writing this book because I am sick and tired of being sick and tired. Everyone living in abuse feels this way, even if you don't realize your situation is abusive. Of this I am certain. You need to know that living a life dictated by abuse is not okay, and you can move away from and beyond this. If you have children, even adult children, you owe it to yourself and them. What a gift you will give.

I grew up in a household with parents and siblings who constantly fought and had no boundaries. A closed door meant nothing. Privacy and respect did not exist. Everyone in my family felt they could do and say whatever they wanted, as harshly as they wanted, without any consequences. I have spent my life being threatened both verbally and physically, shamed, demeaned, humiliated, and intimidated through rage, derogatory language, and disregard. Face-to-face encounters always depleted any energy I had, but recently, most of my abuse has been via destructive emails, phone calls, and voicemails. I've been threatened that if I didn't behave or cease standing up for myself, I'd be sued, destroyed, lose everything, and end up in the streets, homeless.

My abusers always believed they were not abusive because, other than a handful of significantly traumatic physical attacks in my childhood, I have not suffered physical abuse as an adult. I've heard "I never hit you," as if it somehow made their treatment acceptable. This was how they vindicated their behavior to themselves. During a rage, their eyes would go black and blank. Many times, I felt they were going to become physically violent, and in those moments felt my life was in danger. Yet the abusers truly believed they did not inflict any pain or fear, did not break

35

invisible bones or crush my spirit when they attacked then remained self-righteous in their stance of superiority. It was psychologically threatening and I lived in isolation because I didn't know how to reach out for help. The imbalance of power and control terrorized my sense of sanity. It was a debilitating way to live, damaging my spirit and profoundly affecting every aspect of my life. All I ever wished for was peace, yet my life was filled with the madness of abuse going on all around me. And this was happening while I was trying to grow up, live my life, have relationships, and pursue my career. The trauma interfered with any attempt on my part to thrive.

My abusers used anger as a method to gain power and control in order to keep me in my assigned place. Those who perpetrated the abuse toward me were driven by an all-consuming rage and anxiety. In my conscious attempts to understand the anger and rage, I was made to feel wrong for questioning the abusive behavior. My feelings and words would be cut off. **Fault-finding** was one of the many ways the cycle of abuse started for me. It made me feel insane because I could never understand why I was at fault, or why the abuser was making such cruel accusations. It was horrible to always be assigned the role of the failure. Another abusive method was to twist the reality of any situation so I became the one who was always wrong, belittled, and manipulated. My life had been spent navigating around land mines. Often, however, I couldn't wait for the detonations, so eager to get them over with.

The mindset of verbal and emotional abusers: 100% your fault, 0% accountability on theirs. That will be the score of abuse every single time. My abusers never communicated *with* me about their rages and the accusations they made. When I would ask for proof or verification of what they accused me of doing, they never followed through. It was their sense of entitlement and it was beneath them to prove anything. After all, they were always

36

right. I've always felt that if my abusers were to share their thoughts, they would have to see their irrational behavior and would not come out looking good. Because of their **narcissism**, that will never happen. How *dare* I question their integrity or morality? Their rigidity against taking responsibility covers for their cowardice, or arrogance.

Talking to my abusers always made me feel like I was going insane. Since I was always prey to the attacks, my defenses were worn down, and I bought into the insanity often. I found myself **fixing**: trying to calm, placate, and nurture, or just stay out of the way. When I realized there was nothing I could do, I withdrew because I was always defeated and knew what was coming next, resigned to being ineffective. I merely existed. My ability to think clearly became impossible because I accepted and took the blame for the attacks coming at me. I immediately went into survival mode. At times, I would give up the fight in my attempts to stop the abuse. This would cause my abusers to escalate due to my withdrawal. I knew I couldn't stop what was about to happen and in exhaustion, didn't try. I usually found myself resigned to the fact that I was going to be abused and was powerless to stop it, for if I resisted in these moments, it only made things worse. I would eventually relent and claim the supposed offenses just to end the encounter. I always thought it was easier that way, until I began to understand its high cost to my health, spirit, and soul.

I was confronted about anything and everything—even breathing too loudly—yet when I questioned *their* actions, they attacked, denied, or completely withdrew in order to not have a conversation. When I would try to show them the craziness of their behaviors, they would either ignore my voice and feelings or change the direction of the attack to avoid taking responsibility for their words. The abuse I experienced was denied and the abusers never took responsibility. Denial that the behavior was abusive was always in the forefront, and I felt alone in my survival. They always had a long list of behaviors I inflicted on them, and it didn't matter if the infraction happened years earlier, it was brandished as if it had happened the day before. I could never move on from my supposed transgressions—which I heard about over and over again—because the method was crucial to their power and control over me. It kept me trapped in place.

There would be conversations where I felt I was being heard, understood, and recognized as an individual, only to have the supposed understanding disregarded in the next encounter. The withdrawal was never done without first letting me know that everything was my fault. My abusers had **deliberate chronic forgetting syndrome**, at my expense. I can remember throughout my life, I would hold on to any tender gesture from my abusers like I had just been given the greatest gift in the world. However, the kindness never lasted, and I would continue the search for those rare pockets of time. In the good moments, I desperately wanted to believe that all was finally good with the world, though my history told me it was not. My insides would scream, *Danger, danger, danger!* I knew better than to believe. My fantasies would be crushed by reality. This was the delicate dance of abuse I was always trying to perfect, always tripping over my feet.

I believe my abusers were abused by, or witnessed abuse by, people they loved. Some were severely neglected, unable to detach and grow independently as individuals. This is not to excuse their behavior, make light of its impact on me, or justify what they do or did in any way. They were never taught the tools of self-soothing or anger management. Or, they were so lost in their internal turmoil that they, too, were unable to escape. This was the role modeling they had. There seems a fine line between **love** and abuse when you grow up in it. In my family, this already fine line was very blurred. I grew up thinking abuse was love.

38

My abusers used violence—whether psychological or physical—to protect themselves or assuage their guilt and assert dominance over their target. My personal belief is that this behavior is motivated by both feelings of superiority and either an unwillingness or inability to self-examine. In my situation, the abusers did and do not think they are doing anything wrong, and therefore there is nothing to internally inspect. I believe some abusers feel they are above the law. The laws and social graces that apply to you and me do not apply to them. This can make the situation deadly.

In some instances, abusers are vulnerable individuals who cover their own insecurities with increasing anger and rage when confronted with them. They cannot look internally into these insecurities or take responsibility for their volatile behavior. Rage and anger are their front. They need to prevent outbursts by controlling those they love. It is their survival instinct.

In my abusive life situation, the motto was to *deny, deny, deny.* This is how we survived. I believe the only way abusers can get better is to take responsibility for their actions. Taking responsibility for hurting the ones they loved didn't exist in my abusive cycle. I had to personally get to a place where I could connect with the root cause as to why my people abuse. It was a difficult place for me to get to and to understand in my own personal way. I had to get conscious of all that was happening around me as well as my own role in the cycle. Until I got to that point, I participated daily in keeping it going, as my own abusive ways were still active.

I still struggle with the language to describe what happened, so clear in my head, but muffled when the words come out of my mouth. I didn't know how to explain what I felt or what was happening. How do you explain madness, especially if you were a child when it began? It's important to remember that children feel so much and sometimes are unable to express their emotions. What they are going through in abuse is too complicated for their young thinking and verbal skills. Their survival skills are constantly being tested and on heightened alert, always waiting for the next physical, sexual, or psychological blow. Throughout my life, when the venomous words were spewed at me, I was always brought to my knees in devastation and would silently sob. My heart, spirit, and soul would die a little each time a violent physical or emotional attack occurred. They would literally take my breath away, and this reaction can still affect me. As a child, I placated. After all, I had nowhere else to go or a frame of reference.

When I would defend myself, I was verbally and emotionally beaten up more. Sometimes I would try to scream louder, only to escalate the words so carelessly slung my way. I'd duck, roll my eyes, go into **fight-or-flight** mode, but mostly I would become very tired. (Notice the theme of exhaustion.) So frustrated and beaten down, I would give up any hope of being heard or acknowledged. This is how my abusers would "win" the argument and avoid having to take any responsibility for their cruel words.

In a constant state of hyper-vigilance, I was always waiting, always on guard, reacting and surviving. The uncertainty kept me that way, and it was exhausting. The fight or flight reaction was a protective layer I developed at a young age so I could read the signs, predict the danger, and shut down my heart and spirit when the cruel words and actions became overwhelming. I spent much of my life feeling intense fear when an explosion would occur and always felt helpless to stop it. I tried to stay numb to what was happening by using drugs and alcohol in my teens and twenties, but that kind of **escapism** only made things worse. My thoughts were disorganized and I often felt agitated and helpless. At times I have been fearful for my life. Anger was my constant companion; that, and shame.

Psychological abuse can seriously interfere with your sense of self, emotional growth, and development. The field of psychotherapy has many diagnoses to describe how abuse manifests in the psyche. For our purposes, I have changed the word "disorder" to "reaction" because I believe we develop these brilliant strategies for our own survival. There is strength in them, not weakness. I firmly believe we are not disorders, but survivors. We are reacting to our abuse.

I would, for example, have **somatic reactions** during and after abusive episodes. I got chest pains, my heart would beat rapidly and wildly, and at times I would get sharp pains coming from my heart to my left shoulder, arm, and neck area. My breathing would become labored as my fists tightened. At times, I would go into full-blown panic attacks. In my youth, when overwhelmed by my own emotionality while in an abusive episode, I would pass out. As I grew, I stayed because I really did love my family, and the high price I paid has been my **post-traumatic stress** reactions to life, which can come and go. Post-traumatic stress symptoms may be more frequent when things are traumatic in general, or when reminded of the past. You may see a report on the news about a rape and feel overcome by memories of your own assault. I do not diagnose anyone with PTSD. The purpose of explaining this is to let you know that you are not crazy.

I often wondered if I was having a heart attack, especially as I got older. The **anxiety** I walked around with on a daily basis had a tremendous impact on my body, mind, and spirit. I once had a panic attack so severe I was certain it was a heart attack. When I called a hospital emergency room, a wonderful, kind woman explained what was happening and walked me through the panic attack step-by-step. She gave me tools to calm myself. Once I realized what I was experiencing, I would remind myself of the cause of my agitation, that it was not my fault. I was reacting to abuse. I would quiet my mind with things like taking a walk, or working out. I would take deep breaths, in and out, in and out, while acknowledging that I was having a panic attack and feeling intense anxiety. Slowly I was able to calm myself down. This was difficult, as my abuse was all around and I never knew when it would attack. Anxiety takes a real toll on your body—it only makes sense that it would react to your abuse this way.

I always felt off balance, like Wile E. Coyote in the cartoon. The Road Runner would swoop in from nowhere and smash a hammer over the coyote's head, leaving him bewildered, baffled, and confused. You could see the stars coming out of the coyote's head, disoriented by the attack. "Beep, beep!" Off the Road Runner would go. The onslaught always coming at me was that quick and effective. The Road Runner had it down to a science. Yet, the coyote kept coming back for more, so sure in his conviction that he would be able to catch the Road Runner, over and over again. This was my cycle of abuse. I kept coming back for more, so certain I could catch and fix my abusers. I never quite knew what set them off, and like the coyote, I was confused. But how could I feel anything but confused? Catching me off guard and absolving themselves of responsibility for their behavior was their goal. What a crock—but I didn't know that then.

I had to come to the understanding that every time I went through an abusive episode, the internal impact on my system was huge. Because words don't actually break bones or leave visible scars, it was hard for me to get to the place where I understood that the ramifications of the abuse were far-reaching. It's hard to comprehend something that leaves no obvious proof of its destruction.

However, since my mother's death, I have come to understand something else: I desperately wanted to leave the abuse cycle but don't think I would have. I couldn't abandon and leave my mother's side, even though I was becoming depleted of energy and desperately wanted out. I stayed in her abuse along with her own capacity to abuse me and endured. I remained until the day she died. It was a choice that came from somewhere so deep inside me I didn't even know I was making it. I believe this is because I was so young when it started and didn't know anything else. Let me state emphatically, it was not a conscious choice to be abused. No one consciously chooses abuse. I always knew what I was living was wrong. I really did want to leave and get away... I just didn't know how to get through a life of being disempowered over and over again. I was living in a family in which each member had their own definition of survival and was casting it out to the world. I had to change the language of my own abuse and replace it with words of encouragement and empowerment. I needed to remove myself from being a target. I had to become my own parent.

It is with that knowledge I can join each and every one of you with how difficult it is to understand, acknowledge, and leave abuse. There are many reasons we stay. Hopefully I can help you to understand why you stay and how to take the steps needed to leave. My wish is that, through my journey and understanding, you can begin to find strength and courage. Or, if you choose to stay, understand why you are making that choice. This book is also for those who have gotten out, yet still carry the internal scars because they don't know how to talk about it.

I will convey what I know professionally and personally about psychological abuse. Each definition depends on personal experience, so put your own reality in place of mine when our experiences differ....This book is about our commonality.

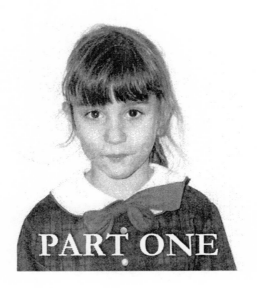

*"The first time someone shows you
who they are, believe them."*

~ Maya Angelou ~

CHAPTER ONE
THE HOLES IN THE STREET

Humor has been my salvation, much of it
sarcasm. Sometimes I use humor in telling this
story. I try to be able to laugh *with* myself
when I fall instead of beating myself up with
harsh internal criticism.

THE HOLES IN THE STREET

How do you catch a cloud and pin it down?
How do you keep a wave upon the sand?
How do you hold a moonbeam in your hand?
~ "Maria," The Sound of Music ~

When *The Sound of Music* came out in 1965, my parents were divorcing. That year, I saw it too many times to count, fantasizing that Maria would come and take me away; I wanted her to be my mommy. Coincidentally, Portia Nelson, who played Sister Berthe in the film, composed the most important piece of writing in my life, a poem titled *Autobiography in Five Short Chapters*. It helped me confront my inner demons and led me to take a look at my own personal values, self-esteem, and worth. This poem changed my life. Portia, I thank you for your brilliance and your insight into the dark, deep hole. I thank you for the gift of this poem. I am grateful for its words, words that are simple and powerful. This poem helped me understand I was stuck; not taking responsibility for my own reality had caused me to tumble back into the darkness time and time again. From both in the depths of the hole and while looking triumphantly down into it, I must have read this poem a million times. I use it in my therapeutic practice. It is my analogy to my own personal growth and healing and integral to the philosophy of this book.

From *Autobiography in Five Short Chapters*

Chapter One

I walk down the street.
There is a deep hole in the sidewalk
I fall in.
I am lost ... I am helpless.
It isn't my fault.
It takes me forever to find a way out.

"Shit," I think. "It happened again."

"How the hell did I end up on the bottom of this hole? Have I ever left the bottom of this hole? Why does this keep happening? Poor me!

"No, I'm not going to say that anymore. It's useless and does not help. I'm so tired of being at the bottom of this hole. Okay, I'm going to put up a ladder. That makes sense. It will make it easier to climb out of the darkness. Up, up, up…Shit, I fell back again.

"Okay, I'll take two steps up and see how that feels. So far, so good. Very shaky. Need a stronger ladder. Breathe! Okay, I'll try another step.

"Damn, I slipped and now I am back at the bottom. How will I ever get out of this hole? Well, I did make it two steps up. I'll try again and maybe I can make it up three. Careful, it's scary. Up one, up two, up three. Here I am on step three.

"Mom called last night…BOOM, back down to the bottom. Ouch, that hurts.

"Get up Deb, you can do this.

"Up one, up two, up three…"

I learned falling back into the hole was a reality, for I didn't have the strength nor the tools to keep me from falling. So I decided to get some. It wasn't easy. You can't buy them at a store. That really made me mad. I just wanted to go to the store, like Home Depot, and pick up some tools for my survival. It would have saved so much time and money. Seriously, "The Emotional Tool Store." What a concept! Pick an emotion, pick a tool.

My toolbox wouldn't be a toolbox at all, but a backpack to make it easier to carry my tools out of the hole and maybe a fanny pack to keep some of my emotions in a containable but easily accessible space. High powered flashlights for illumination. A clean air purifier to make breathing easier. Extra filters. Lots of water. Hammer—for my anger. Cordless screw gun to tighten up all my loose nuts and bolts. An extra drill-bit, because there are a lot of screws loose. Mortar to fill in the holes of my brick house. I can keep out the monsters and ghosts that way. Air freshener for stinky thoughts. A dustless vacuum to suck up all the "icky." Large garbage can. Monkey glue because it sounds really strong and I love monkeys. Paint and a brush to begin a new landscape. Rope and a ladder to help me climb out of the hole. Four all-season tires so when I am out I can drive the hell away! If the visual of my fists can help you here, take them and begin your fight out of the hole. Take my fists for strength and empowerment, not violence.

You get the point. Problem is: the tools don't magically appear, yet they are all around us. You can learn them through reading, education, and professional help. You can gain them through loving friends or that mentor who showed up in your life, maybe a childhood teacher whose kindness you will always remember. Sitting on the bottom of the hole, I slowly learned which tools were worth keeping in my backpack. It was shaky at first, so new was each stride. With each step forward, my backpack became lighter and lighter. Each time I would fall back down, I would sit with the fall and figure out what led to my slip. I would embrace its impact. I would be kind to myself through my journey out of the darkness. Instead of loud critical thinking, I began to quiet the noise in my head. Lo and behold, I slowly started climbing up and out instead of constantly falling to the bottom.

"Up one, up two, up three. Fell again, but this time only to the first step. At least I'm still on the ladder!" For every two steps forward, you may take three steps back. For every five steps forward, you may take four steps back. Breathing becomes easier and you are less frustrated when you do fall because you are gaining the tools necessary to climb. You begin to embrace the ladder, because that is where the learning is. I still work on this today because falling back is a reality. It becomes more about how long we are willing to stay down. And in all honesty, there are still days when I stay down and am unable to find the ladder. But now at least I know when I am down at the bottom and don't stay there very long.

From *Autobiography in Five Short Chapters*

Chapter Two

I walk down the same street.
There is a deep hole in the sidewalk.
I pretend I don't see it.
I fall in again.
I can't believe I am in the same place
but, it isn't my fault.
It still takes a long time to get out.

Denial is a defense mechanism that exists for a person who is faced with a situation or information that is impossible to accept. They are unable to deal with what has ensued, even when shown it is real. Denial manifests in many different forms. One can deny completely that an unpleasant event occurred. Others may minimize the seriousness of the event. Denying and minimizing is common for those of us living in abuse. We tend to downplay the seriousness of what we are living and **rationalize** what is happening in order to survive. Your abuser may admit an event or situation occurred, but they are experts at taking little to no responsibility. What is consistent is they repeat the same behavior pattern and project blame on everyone else, usually on you.

For me, it worked something like this. When my mother would go into her rages and spews of verbal violence at me, I would rationalize the encounter by telling myself it wasn't so bad and make myself believe that my mother loved me. The outside world kept telling me how much my mother loved me, so it had to be true. I justified abusive behaviors so I could endure. In other instances, I kept telling myself if I could just be who she wanted me to be, and I never knew what that was, she would stop yelling at me, see me and want to get to know me. I was sure if I stuck with it, I could get her to love me.

On the flip side, for those being abused, I believe denial exists as a brilliant survival technique. Forgetting is easier than remembering. It is less painful and does not require any work. It is easily accessible for those who truly need it. It saves lives. It works. It is survival, but there is a heavy cost. I spent so much of my life pretending I did not see what was in front of me. I believe it is how I minimized for myself the severity of what I was living as a way to survive. My life eventually became so painful that I spent years not being able to accept, or cope with my reality. To survive, I had to break away from what was happening and the truths of my family. My abilities amazed even me. When an abusive episode occurred, I was able to come to terms with the abuse quickly so the outside world would not see, act as if nothing had happened and somehow convince myself that everything was okay. But internally I was a mess, always.

I believe the never-ending impact of the chaos around me necessitated this minimization and denial. It was just easier. I still have times when denying what is happening around me is easier than seeing it, for it is often so hard to wrap my brain around the mess. Denial, in its absurd wisdom, kept me safe and, at times, still does. It shielded me from my reality and memories that were scary, dark, and internally deadly, especially as a child. It helped keep me alive. So I continued down the same street, still plummeting into the hole. I finally understood I would continue to fall until I started getting honest with myself. I needed to start really feeling what was happening to me in order to figure out how to move beyond and away.

Tired of being at the bottom of the hole, surrounded by all the dark and loneliness, I needed to make a shift in my behavior and attitude, and the beginning of this awareness told me I was ready. Once you know better, you can't go back. The time had come for me to start healing, find my empowerment, and move forward. Denial was a tool I no longer needed. And I did thank it for its usefulness, for its presence. I put my denial to rest as best I could and let it know I would call on it when needed. I thanked it for helping keep me safe all those years.

With denial put to rest, I knew I had hit the bottom of the hole, because I was no longer pretending it wasn't there. I became tired of ending up in the same place over and over again. It was redundant, and my determination to end the pain and suffering became stronger than my denial. I knew my story, my reality; the abuse wasn't my fault. I knew this intellectually, and now it was time for my heart to catch up. I call this the **heart-mind connection**. I began to embrace the pain and fear and use it to guide me. As I went inside myself, I defined the chaotic pieces of my spirit and soul to help me understand what was going on and how to repair the damage. I knew my **inner child** needed a hug, and I started creating a protective parent for myself to keep her safe. I told her we would go on this journey together, extending my hand to her. I gave myself the gift of time to trek out of the hole and into the unknown.

When I embraced my child, I found she was lost, scared, and lonely, filled with rage and so much sadness. Her fists wouldn't unclench, even for me. In my early forties, I created a healing place in my mind where I could go when the fear would overwhelm. It was a king-size bed in the brilliant blue sky, with puffy cumulonimbus clouds and a soft, soothing sun. On the bed was a thick, warm, and wonderful down comforter, with pillows all around. I was surrounded by my cats and the dog I did not yet have. I felt warm and safe in this bed. It comforted my nerves and calmed my heart. As I look back on my fantasy now, I am intrigued by the unconscious desire for comfort in my fantasy—I choose a down comforter. This is the bed I then bought and have slept in for the last twelve years.

Once I found my safe place, I began talking to my inner child. It was then I realized no one had ever stood up for or protected her. My heart broke, for she had endured so much. I let her know that we were going to do this together. I stopped feeling all alone. Within the safety of this new tool—still fragile, but comforting—an internal conversation of conviction toward healing began to take place. I was scared, but was protecting my little girl as an adult. I continued on, keeping the fear away from my child, who had endured enough distress. I started growing up.

From *Autobiography in Five Short Chapters*

Chapter Three

I walk down the same street.
There is a deep hole in the sidewalk.
I see it is there.
I still fall in ... it's a habit.
My eyes are open
I know where I am.
It is my fault.
I get out immediately.

As I continued my journey, I continued to fall. Though I ended up back in the hole time and time again, I was learning how to both climb out and accept that falling back was a habit. I was responsible for unlearning this behavior, so I stopped beating myself up when I fell. Instead, I sat quietly to pay attention to what was going on around me. Sometimes I would curl up and stay stuck. But with each fall, the days, hours, and minutes began to shorten. I understood when my unhealthy survival strategies no longer served me, and began replacing them with better coping skills. I no longer sat in the darkness. I was fighting through it and winning. I built a wonderful village of support with friends who understood my journey and no longer tried to move forward alone. My strength became stronger than the abuse. I embraced each fall back as a learning opportunity and knew if I could just hold on to my forward journey, no matter how hard it became, I was on my way towards the light and out of the darkness.

When I told my child she could let go of the fears and rest, you should have seen the looks she gave me! At first, she wasn't buying any of it, and my internal war escalated. Fighting yourself is quite an experience—one I believe is based in fear of the unknown. I hated the sense of worthlessness that had been instilled in me, but I didn't know any other way to feel. To let go of all you know is very scary, and giving up the **comfort in the discomfort** is overwhelming. So there stood my child with her fists, asking questions: *How can you ask me to give up my defenses? How do you expect to keep us safe? How can you protect me when you allowed this to happen in the first place?* The objections screaming from her were of a little girl too frightened to let go, who continuously, and falsely, blamed herself for the abuse. It was the yin-yang, back and forth of my emotions up in arms. But I pushed forward, even though my child's fists tightened during this time of trauma. She was furious at my interference and didn't want to change. She took her time to trust me and believe we can do this.

As we persevered, I let her know I would protect her. I unlocked her fists and massaged them, just as I had my own. Together, we got rid of all the knots and bulges that had formed. I let her know she could sleep, told her I would ask for her help if I needed it. I told her she was smart, beautiful, and a gift to me as I hugged and nurtured her. I stroked her hair, as my second grade teacher once had, so *knowingly*, and I told her how much I loved her. When I heard her sigh with relief, I put her under the covers and lovingly tucked her in. I did every cliché and fantasy I ever had about how I wanted my mother to mother me. I loved my child with all her defenses, strength, spirit, and—most of all—her fists. I honored her experience. I let her off the hook, and curled up with her while she fell asleep. And for the first time in my life, we fell into a quiet, peaceful rest. I was a good mommy.

I began to honor my experience. As I tried to figure out how to get up from the bottom of the hole, I kept telling myself I was on my way to healing and health, even if I thought I didn't have a clue as to what I needed to do. I often fell back to the bottom. But in my determination to no longer allow things out of my control to control me, I did not give up. Becoming an expert at challenging myself, I used positive self-talk that told me I would figure it out, even when I fell back. I personally found empowerment through exercise and focusing more deliberately on my breathing. Dealing with abuse through logical thought— which I'd tried to do my whole life—is impossible. Abuse is illogical. You can't make sense out of something that does not and never will. Trying to make the irrational rational is absolutely *futile*. What a waste of time! I still work on this one when the abuse escalates and I want to fix it. I can't. I never have been able to. I never will be.

Now, when I fall back into the hole, my ladder is sturdy and strong. My backpack is filled with my emotional tools and my legs are well-muscled. The climb out, while it still remains challenging, is becoming easier. My fists pull me up in positive determination instead of fending off an abusive reality. It has been hard work, and at times it still is, but I will reach freedom. Through the process, I remind myself to thank my inner child, to let her know how appreciative I am of all her hard work in surviving the madness, in building up the defenses that kept us safe.

From *Autobiography in Five Short Chapters*

Chapter Four

I walk down the same street.
There is a deep hole in the sidewalk.
I walk around it.

Once I knew the hole was there, I understood it was now up to me to change it. I was able to slowly start defining a **new normal**. At first I didn't know what that looked like, but I was certainly getting clearer on what I *didn't* want. That on its own brought a sense of freedom and relief. I was learning I no longer needed to stay stuck in my current reality with my fears. I acknowledged I had the power to keep moving forward. It has taken me time to start creating an adult life with my rules, my boundaries, and my visions. But, as I merged the fantasy with life's realities, I began forming a cohesive self with an **observing ego**.

It took me years to develop my observing ego, or even to know that I needed one. For example,

An observing ego allowed me to step outside myself and take a look at what I was doing. Letting go of my past, I knew I had to start implementing new goals, defined by me with my rules and desires. As I began to form a picture in my mind of my new normal, I was able to start imagining what this fresh reality would be. I envisioned where I wanted to be and what I wanted to do. The greatest part of this journey was that I knew it could evolve as I went until I found the right fit; I now know this is the journey of life, forever changing and growing. There was comfort in knowing that if I didn't like something I tried, I didn't have to do it again. When I found something I liked, I got to nurture it and help it blossom. My reality, defined by me—how perfect! How did I not think of this before?

As my journey kept moving forward, I was learning to listen to the music, literally started washing my hair in the rain, and was laughing from my belly. It didn't matter how long or short these periods would last, I was living them. When abuse lurked back in and I tumbled to the bottom of the hole, I was able to get out. I was surviving, growing and changing my story one step, one minute, and one day at a time. Some days I did it better than others, but that's okay. I'm human. I say: When you reach this point, throw yourself a fabulous party, one that exemplifies your new normal, with all of your friends there to help you celebrate your growth. You are no longer stuck in the hole, no longer falling in it. And if you do stumble, you now know how to get right back out.

From *Autobiography in Five Short Chapters*

Chapter Five

I walk down another street.

I survived. You too can survive your journey out. I am in the light, though every once in a while I still have to change the bulb. You can find the light. I've grown. You can grow. I've changed my story and so can you. I've changed my life and so can you. I am beautiful and so are you.

59

Now that I am out of the hole, at least most of the time, I have learned that life is full of ups and downs, highs and lows. I also know now I am in control. Losing control and giving up my power is something I still work very hard to properly negotiate as I continue to strengthen my understanding of life's rules and boundaries. I accept the reality of my past, and when the outside abuse comes at me, I continue to nurture my child through her trauma, for the abuse is not ours anymore. She can still be feisty and reactive, but I support her responses while fostering her confidence that I will protect her and keep her out of harm's way. I am also getting better at reaching out and asking for help. I try not to do it alone anymore.

My little girl still works to believe my adult will become the parent for whom she has longed her whole life. I have given myself the gift of myself, which has allowed for a more meaningful life—allowed, in fact, for a life at all. I have now merged with my child and formed a cohesive identity, at least on most days. When the dark, scary noise enters my head, I have a better grip on how to handle and quiet it. I have kept and honored my story, my reality; I just don't have to live it anymore. I am standing taller, with a sense of pride at the hard work I have been doing. I continue to unclench my fists, knowing they are there if I need them, but I can relax the muscles as I become whole. I am humbled by this journey of letting go.

Another analogy I use in my work with self is the minefield of my internal structure, which can be difficult to navigate. Before these analogies were a part of my toolbox, I could be very demanding in my relationships. I wanted others to fix me. For many decades, I had the fantasy that somehow my parents would repair things, that they would see the errors of their ways, correct the wrongs, become the loving parents of my fantasy. My wish and need was for my friends and the men I dated to remove the land mines, pull me out of and fill my holes.

Somehow, I thought that would solve my problems, but all it did was trap me, my friends, and my boyfriends in a draining cycle. My **abandonment fears** always took hold, and the relationships were like rugs covering craters, built on expectations born from the magical thinking of a child.

When I started, I thought filling up all those dark holes was my journey. *That* didn't work, as we know, but I now have an impressive collection of shovels. Then, I thought I had to detonate each land mine in order to find my eventual peace. Well, that didn't work either. Once I realized that, the next step I took was to honor these holes and landmines and learn to traverse, not rid myself of, them.

In the spirit of Nelson's poem, each chapter of this book contains two sections:

In the Trenches: Here I share details of the memories and feelings I have about living in abuse and my journey out. *The "text" associated with the memories and feeling is NOT shaded.*

The View From 10,000 Feet: This is my professional, clinical perspective and observations about what we experience. As a clinical social worker,   I understood intellectually what was happening even if I was not yet strong enough to respond. I describe my lessons learned on the journey toward recovery while sharing my steps toward health, freedom, and happiness. *The "text" associated with my professional clinical prospective IS shaded.*

Through my words, my journey, and my tools, I offer you a chance to find your own voice. I validate your experience with the hope of guiding you to begin your own journey towards freedom and away from the constant collision course. You no longer need to just survive your existence. I know how hard it is to get out once you are in. From this place of sympathetic wisdom, I ask you to dig deep so you can begin to understand how abuse has affected your life and stop believing that you participated in it. Abuse happened to you. You did not create it, cause it, or agree to let it happen. Your abuser took that choice away the minute you were first abused. Know this, believe this, and carry that knowledge with you as you journey away from abuse to find your real, authentic self.

Humor has been my salvation, much of it sarcasm. Sometimes I use humor in telling this story. I try to be able to laugh *with* myself when I fall instead of beating myself up with harsh internal criticism. I exaggerate that I have been in therapy for 999 years. It reminds me that this is hard work and it does not happen overnight. It truly is baby steps. It is the holes in the street. You find you are finally climbing out, and the next minute you are back on the bottom. Believing in yourself, and the affirmation of this over and over again, begins the journey out and away. It is constant conscious awareness that when you take steps back, you need to reboot and continue forward. Eventually, you will find the street with smaller holes where the fall is not so dark, or as deep. Those holes are life's lessons; climbing is coping.

CHAPTER TWO
INTUITION TOLD ME SO

I had acquired some tools, however, by my fiftieth birthday. My mother, by now in her late seventies, was visiting to help me celebrate.

INTUITION TOLD ME SO

Intuition is a spiritual faculty and does not
explain, but simply points the way.
~ Florence Scovel Shinn ~

There were many situations during my life when I tried to make my mother happy and couldn't succeed. One event in particular stays with me to this day: her sixtieth birthday. I was in my early thirties, and her relationship with Jack was new. My siblings and I decided to throw her a surprise birthday party. We were excited, worked hard, and managed to keep it null. We invited people we knew, those who had been friends with her all our lives. All the people we knew who went way back with our mother. She thought she was going to Jack's house to get ready for an evening out. After what was a wonderful "surprise," my mother needed a shower and I went into the bathroom with her. What I got from her in the bathroom devastated me.

"How could you do this to me?" She exploded, "You didn't invite the right people. It's going to hurt my business relationships. People are going to be angry with me. How could you be so insensitive? Look at all the problems you've created for me."

What I heard and felt was, "You're a failure. Can't you ever do anything right? You're worthless and I don't love you." I sat on the sink counter, crushed. I wanted to curl up and die, yet remained paralyzed. I couldn't leave the bathroom. She could not see my devastation. At this point in my life I had not gained the tools I needed to deal with her unkindness, her assaults. I did not have the strength to take the hurt, so I just went numb. The problem with the numbness, however, was the hurt always found a way in eventually.

I had acquired some tools, however, by my fiftieth birthday. My mother, by now in her late seventies, was visiting to help me celebrate. I woke up that morning, the day before we would elect Barack Obama president. My mother was impressed with the young senator from Illinois. She liked what he stood for and became a tireless volunteer for his presidential campaign, going to the Iowa Caucus and the Inauguration in Washington. She watched this African-American president enter office with much pride.

As I came downstairs that morning, my mother was already in her daily frenzy. I thought she would make a big deal about me, her daughter, turning fifty. After all, she had flown out to be with me. She was in one of her anxious moods and could not slow down. I attempted unsuccessfully to calm her, then took my dog for a walk so I would not be an outlet for her anxiety. When I returned, she still would not acknowledge my birthday. No hugs, no words of sentiment, no nothing. I was shocked, but this time I had tools. I said, "Mom, It's my fiftieth birthday. Fifty years ago today you bore me from your loins. You had your little girl. Wish me a happy birthday and give me a hug."

She could not do this, so caught up in her anxiety and needs. Her need that morning was to get to the local Obama headquarters where we would spend the day making phone calls to make sure people were getting out to vote. Important, I agree. This was a big election. But it was my birthday and I wasn't backing down. "Mother, wish me a happy birthday and give me a hug." She was baffled. I was interfering with the noise in her head. I said it again when she did not respond. Eventually I received a very tentative hug, a quick pat on the back and a brief happy birthday and then she very forcefully told me to get ready and that we were late.

Oh well, so much for turning fifty, but this time it was different. I had gained tools to deal with my mother. Her behavior still hurt, always hurt, but I had learned how not to personalize her dismissive stance. I knew she loved me. I knew she adored me. I was able to laugh at the absurdity of the situation. I was able to hug myself and say "Welcome fifty." I was able to let it go. We spent the day at Obama headquarters making phone calls. I gave my day to my mother. It was okay. I was not devastated. It just was what it was. Okay, I was a little sad. Well, maybe a lot sad, but I didn't let it devastate and destroy me. After all, I did what I could do, and I was on my way to having a new kind of relationship with my mother, one with firm emotional boundaries in place that would enable the positive attributes of our connection to shine through. This was in November; by June she was gone.

Impossible! Not that she was killed or that she is dead. I knew that was going to happen. The impossible comes in how to deal with it, how to understand it and attempt to have it make sense. How is my mother—a woman so vital, energetic, and compassionate to the outside world—dead?

I was not there, but from what I was told it was a beautiful morning after what had been a long spell of rainy, cloudy days. My mom, as usual, was up bright and early, living each second of the day with her inexhaustible energy and lust for life. She never wanted to miss a minute. She was off to the golf course and Jack decided to join her. Not to golf, or even drive the cart. He was in very poor health and could barely walk. He hadn't been allowed to drive in years and had a home health care assistant to drive for him. My mother was excited any time Jack showed motivation to participate in life, which wasn't often.

They were on the second hole of the golf course, and my mom was going to retrieve her ball. The only thing certain is she left the keys in the cart. I don't think it would have ever occurred to her that Jack would attempt to drive. The next thing that happened, according to a newspaper article, was an eyewitness saw Jack driving approximately fifteen miles an hour, which is as fast as a golf cart can go. My seventy-seven year-old mother's tiny frame was crushed. Did he get behind the wheel, or reach his arm and leg over from the passenger side when he made the decision to drive?

My cousin reported that a nineteen-year-old employee at the golf course saw my mother on the ground, yelled to a friend to call 911, and ran to her. He knelt down and stayed with her until help arrived. He said she was extremely stressed and breathing weakly. She had cuts on her face and told him, "Someone hit me." She attempted to lift her head and he told her to keep still. He noticed that her ankle was fractured and told her to relax, that an ambulance was on the way. He asked what happened. She stated, "My husband hit me." She then told him she did not want to be a paraplegic.

At first I didn't want to know the extent of all her injuries, my mom's little body crushed to death. The images I had of her lying on the second hole and in the hospital so torn apart were just too painful, but eventually I learned from someone who was at the hospital that her left foot was almost severed at the ankle, her left femur had a compound fracture, left hip bone was moved to where her spine would be. She had broken ribs and a collapsed lung, was given fifteen pints of blood, and had internal bleeding all over the doctors were unable to stop. And yet, my mother fought, for eight hours, through surgery after surgery to find and stop the bleeding, fought until her last moment of breath.

I woke that same morning feeling off; you know one of those days everything makes you angry and you don't have a clue why? My anger was getting the best of me and I was lashing out at everyone. I was at work thousands of miles away from my mom and my cell phone was off. When I got off work and turned my phone back on, I noticed several calls from my younger brother, who lived near our mom. I decided to call him back later because I had to get to the hardware store for toilet parts. You see, she was coming to visit me the next week to celebrate her seventy-eighth birthday, and the guest toilet was broken. I needed to fix it for my mother; my brother could wait.

After fixing the toilet, my friend Barney and I decided to go watch the sunset at a golf course. (That's right, I said *golf course*.) Still oblivious to all that had happened to my mother, I was looking forward to enjoying the beautiful summer evening. We had just gotten our drinks and went out to the back deck to sit, look at the mountains, watch the golfers, and take in the sunset. My cell phone began to vibrate and I saw one call after another from my brother. I had not heard the phone ringing for the last hour-and-a-half, but now there were dozens of messages. Something was wrong. I turned to Barney and said, "My life is about to change." The feeling of dread that wrapped around me since I woke finally made sense. It was difficult to make the call, knowing whatever he was going to tell me would alter my life forever. The impending doom and unsettled anger I had been feeling all day told me so.

The first voicemail said, "Mom's been in an accident and hurt her foot. I'm on my way to the hospital." The progression of messages became more hysterical:

"She's bad. You need to get here immediately."

"This is bad."

"She's in serious condition." *Serious?* I couldn't comprehend how it got from "hurt her foot" to "serious." He had said more in the messages, but those words remain in the fog of my memory. A numb place opened its doors and took me in, locking away all I could not grasp.

As this was going on, the sky above me began to darken, a storm fast approaching. I swear this is true. I knew it would be impossible to fly out of town on a moment's notice. The reality of what was happening was crazy. I couldn't breathe. Barney grabbed me, put me in his car and drove me to my other brother's house, who lived in the same town. During the drive, my overwhelming sense of losing my mom grew with each call.

In my brother's living room, I was choked and scared, trying to will this nightmare away. My panic began to escalate. All I wanted to do was go home and be with her. Mother and daughter: that unbreakable bond between women—whether good, bad, or indifferent. Though she portrayed toughness to the outside world, I knew she was scared. I knew she needed me there, the only person with whom she could be vulnerable. It was emotionally devastating to carry all the stories of her life, our life, and not be with her in those moments.

I went out to the deck and began calling the hospital. No one there would give me information. Said they couldn't. After all, how did they really know I was her daughter? The situation was exasperating and cruel. Here I was, stuck thousands of miles away, and the hospital, following protocol. The feelings of helplessness and worry made me want to explode. With each call from my younger brother, the crippling uncertainty was becoming more evident, at least to me. I needed to get to her.

We asked a friend who lives near my mother to go to the hospital to help support my brother. Barney took me home so I could pack while he attempted to get me a flight. The storm had halted all air travel in and out of our small mountain town. I would not be able to get a flight out that night.

In my stress, Barney took me to a local bistro for a glass of wine. He was my calming force and I was grateful for his presence. I called our friend just as she arrived at the hospital. In order to get into the area where my mother was being treated, I told her to tell them she was me, her daughter. That, they believed.

With me at her ear, she climbed the hospital stairs, navigated the corridors and found my mother's room. As she entered, she exclaimed, "Oh my God, your mother just coded! Oh my God, your mother is dead!" The words delivered that fast, that quickly, and it was over. She was dead. I remember losing all body control and falling to my knees in the backyard of the bistro, the words, *my mother is dead, my mother is dead*, screaming at deafening decibels inside my head. The next thing I knew, Barney picked me up and ran me out to his car. IMPOSSIBLE! This is not happening. I couldn't feel anything. What the hell was going on?

Jack did it. He killed her. He actually killed her. I had known for the last two years he was going to, never imagining it would be such a horrific "accident." Never imagining her body would be so torn apart. Never imagining her death would be filled with so much fear and pain. But I knew he was going to "accidentally" kill her, told her he was going to, and I begged her to leave. My **intuition** knew; being abused told me so.

There has been so much devastation and sadness since my mother was killed, and rightly so. It was horrendous. In an instant, after so much work to correct a lifetime of holding my breath in abuse, my ability to breathe again became stifled. I felt pulled down and exhausted by the darkness all around me.

I realized that, in dealing with my mother's death and in needing to tell my story of abuse, I was incapable of accessing the tools I had accumulated up to that point. Everything I learned felt lost for a moment. I was experiencing the common post-traumatic stress *reaction* that can follow such a tragic event. All I wanted to do was slow down and walk through the pain of losing my mother. In that moment, and for some time thereafter, I mentally and physically could not do so, and therefore felt alone and lost. Yet I knew in those moments I would not continue to live in abuse and all its secrets. The night she died, I was, quite literally, **done.**

What I did decide to do was stay focused on how my life was getting better, the goals I had for this book, and the collective conversation I wanted to start about abuse. I also acknowledged I was continuing to learn and had just hit what I hoped was a momentary roadblock. I knew I had to slow down and hug my inner child. I was not going to deviate from my plan to tell my secrets, it just meant that for the moment I couldn't do anything. I knew I would stick to my convictions and boundaries, but it was hard. In fact, I knew I would shout it out from the mountaintops as soon as I figured out which mountains to climb.

Revealing my secrets came with the understanding that many would abandon me in my quest to tell. However, I knew, and had to keep reminding myself, that many more would be there to support me. I was not going to choke on something I had not created, and I knew I would keep sharing my story with whoever would listen.

It is not my intention to name people or call them out on the carpet. Due to the tragedy of my mother's death, all involved have had their own journeys. This is my story of how I felt; I don't wish to dwell on it, just tell it as I experienced it. Immediately following my mother's death was the hardest work I have done since I started my healing. It took three months to act, but I was not able to right after her death. All I knew in that moment was there would be an end date. I just wasn't sure when that date would be. So I put one foot in front of the other, taking care of what I believed needed to be, along with what I had no control over, until I could break free.

This is what I knew, but most importantly, what I've learned.

Revealing my secrets came with the understanding that many would abandon me in my quest to tell. However, I knew, and had to keep reminding myself, that many more would be there to support me.

CHAPTER THREE
THE CHAIN STOPS HERE

Before I can tell you about my journey away from abuse, I need to share my parents' stories, as abuse is a cycle that repeats itself through generations until the chain is broken.

THE CHAIN STOPS HERE

Every time you are tempted to react the same old way,
ask if you want to be a prisoner of the past or a pioneer of the future.
~ Deepak Chopra ~

Before I can tell you about my journey away from abuse, I need to share my parents' stories, as abuse is a cycle that repeats itself through generations until the chain is broken. Especially with my family's pathology, I have worked very hard to break this chain. By understanding them, I was able to understand the madness that was my life and how to make the changes necessary for my survival. I am determined the chain of abuse will stop with me.

There is good, bad, and ugly in everything; I like to call it **the whole enchilada**. This is life. It has been my experience living in psychological abuse that I saw the world as all black and all white (all good and all bad), with the darkness usually winning. My life's graph was filled with extreme highs and lows—no middle ground. I still struggle with this one. I needed to allow for some grey and deal with the impact its absence had been having on my life. There are those of you reading this book whose reality may be that there is no good. Constantly dangerous situations may cause you to always be on heightened alert. I don't wish to downplay your experience, and suggest you need to find good where there may be none in your current situation. So read this chapter with an open mind. That said, where there is abuse, it is rarely all darkness. Most abusers don't abuse one hundred percent of the time. For many of us, there are some gifts we've received and periods of light we can hold onto and grow from. The good times, though, contribute to the confusion we feel when we are being abused.

Since my relationship with my father has always been strained, I will focus mostly on my mother, whose impact on my life was the greatest and most difficult. From my father I received my playfulness and creativity, my athleticism, a value on the importance of education, and an appreciation for all kinds of music. He also gave me my favorite quality, my sense of humor with its hint (okay, maybe more than a hint) of sarcasm. I am thankful for these influences. They are very much a part of who I am today. When I really looked at these aspects, the good parts of me slowly began to emerge and I began to understand. Despite everything, as human beings my parents were very bright individuals. They encouraged intelligence and thinking. They were funny, creative, musical, athletic, and loved to travel the world. They gave me wonderful gifts I enjoy to this day. My life experience led me to become a therapist. I have loved my career and the difference I have made in so many lives, especially the lives of children. I am good at it because I know.

In my years of being a clinical social worker, I worked with adult and adolescent sexually-aggressive males as well as children who were removed from the home due to abuse. I have seen the effects of physical, sexual, and emotional violence on those being abused and those who abuse. Based on what I observed, I developed my own theory about how abuse is perpetuated. This is not a scientific study and I have no formal, documented research to back up what I am saying. *I'm just saying.*

It occurred to me that many if not most people who grow up in abusive families do not become adults who abuse—quite the contrary. I believe that at some point in your life you come to a crossroad where you either take a right or left turn. Taking a right turn is the high moral ground where we know that violence and abuse is wrong and would never treat another adult or child that way, despite that being our experience growing up. The biggest tragedy for those who take a right moral turn is that they tend to blame themselves for it happening. **Abuse turned inward** is a self-destructive tendency in which the abused perpetuate the torment by believing they are what the abusers tell them: worthless. In addition to blaming themselves, like me, they may believe if they stay in it long enough, they can get acceptance and love from the abuser. With my clients and myself, I have found the most difficult part of the journey is being able to let ourselves off the hook for the abuse happening.

Those who take a left turn choose to continue to perpetuate violence and abuse. I believe they have lost their ability to form a cohesive self and their conscience is severely compromised, if one exists at all. Some are just born with a missing link in their internal structure. It was extremely difficult for me in my professional practice to make a dent with those who took a left turn. Many learned how to talk the talk of health and healing because the legal system demanded it of them, but it did not stop their abusive ways or abusive thinking. They just became experts at manipulating the system. My co-workers and I called this "sliming the therapist" and "sliming the judges" with their smooth and sophisticated front, just like how they meet the women and men they abuse. I always felt the talk was for the purpose of removing authorities and the legal system from their lives. Abusers can be very smart and seductive. After most sessions, I would turn to another therapist to get de-slimed. To take a left turn means for me that the person has no moral compass or real consciousness of their behavior. I believe teaching someone to have a conscience, in most cases, cannot happen. Where do you reach in to get abusers to take a long, hard look at their behavior when the denial system and lack of a moral compass is stronger than they are?

Know that if you remain in the abuse, without help and willingness on your abuser's part to change, they will never stop and your abuse will continue. And it *will* be passed down to your children in either way described above. The impact on them will follow them through life unless they stop it. I know there are other professionals who will disagree with what I have said here, and that is fine. This is my belief.

My family's story is loud or soft depending on who's telling it. It's a story filled with emotions I don't think there are names for. It's a story of which I no longer wish to be part, but I feel compelled to tell with the hope that it will touch others and help them move forward. It's a story that still brings me much sadness and pain.

My paternal grandparents were a very hardworking couple. My grandfather, a Russian immigrant, was a pharmacist who owned five drug stores which my grandmother ran. Being so unavailable, they never had time for their only child. My father began his life learning he was just in the way of two very busy people. They abandoned, neglected, and were unable to show love to their little boy. My father "died" when he was five, that fragile age when the world is one big playground with all the childlike wonderment of this thing called life. He was emptied and shut down when his parents sent him off to boarding school at this tender age.

My father often told me that when they dropped him off at boarding school, he wrapped his arms around a radiator and clung to it for dear life. He cried and cried in pain and sadness as his parents drove away. After the teachers finally pried his arms from around the radiator, my father says he never cried again, so beaten down by the spirit-crushing reality inflicted upon him by his parents.

They would visit every other Sunday. The school was up at the top of a hill, and when he heard their car coming, he would get physically sick. They would take him into town for a burger, drive him back up, and leave. I once drove out to the school with my father and watched him relive the pain of his childhood from the moment our car reached the bottom of the hill. My heart broke for him as I witnessed his little boy's suffering firsthand, trauma that has followed him throughout his life. His parents' indifference defeated him, so he went numb, the boyhood innocence forever lost. Dead at the age of five. This shaped the man, husband, and father my dad would become.

His father, my grandfather, died when I was four. My grandmother I never felt really loved me. She did not like women, or girls, and showed interest only in the men of our family. This was just one of many messages my young soul received to suggest I was worthless and unworthy. She was also dismissive and unkind towards my mother and maternal grandmother. She did not like them, nor did she like that my mother had married her son. My mother was not good enough for him. There was at least one party during which they were banished from the room. She never had any interest in anything they had to say. Why they allowed it and put up with it, I don't know.

It's interesting to think about my mother's childhood. During the Depression, my maternal grandfather lost everything and had to move the family in with my mother's maternal grandparents. According to the stories she has told me, she grew up feeling unloved by her father and had **idealized** her mother. She talked about a babysitter who terrorized her and would lock her in a closet. When I asked questions about it, she would only say that the moment her mother found out, the babysitter was fired. Problems were solved that easily and without fallout. There is a story there I do not know.

After college, my mother moved out on her own with a friend. Unmarried women did not do that sort of thing at the time. The two of them ended up running back to their homes because the outside world thought they were prostitutes. Her vision of independence was ahead of the times. She then owned a very successful company with four other female pioneers, again, at a time when women did not do that sort of thing.

She lived through World War II, married my father who fought in that war, and lived through the Vietnam War with a son who was becoming the age when the possibility of being drafted was all too real. These experiences, as well as some I don't know, left her in fear with the anxiety of always waiting for the next blow to hit. It was exhausting to watch.

After my mother died, a second cousin told me how every night, my grandmother would draw a bath for herself and make my mother sit in the room with her while she bathed. During these times, she would tell my mother over and over again how painful it was for her to give birth. My mother was an only child who idolized my grandmother, never saying one negative thing about her, unable to get angry with her for anything. I always wondered if it was due to her guilt over the sacrifices my grandmother—a warm, soft, and fuzzy kind of grandma—made for us. She gave up her life and her own happiness to help her daughter and grandchildren.

My maternal grandfather died when my mother was in college. When I was very young, my widowed grandmother met an Englishman named Leslie. They met on the Queen Elizabeth II ocean liner and fell in love. She would visit him in England and New York, and eventually he asked her to marry him. My parents' marriage at that time was falling apart, so my grandmother declined his proposal, choosing instead to devote her life to her daughter and grandchildren. She filled in for my mother often, and was always involved in our lives. She gave the most wonderful back scratches, made scrambled eggs I am still trying to figure out how to replicate, listened, and loved. I turned to her for hugs. (Oh, and she put plastic on our furniture.) It saddens me that she did not marry the love of her life, but I was grateful to have had my *Nana*. I am certain if she had left, I would have withered away. She gave up her life to save mine. I know my mother felt this way, and I think the guilt haunted her throughout her life.

My mother worked tirelessly and was admired by most people she met. She certainly left an impression on the world around her. Most were in awe of her energy and her style. She was noticed when she passed by with her little body, her little face and her large distinctive glasses perched on her little nose. She seized life, refusing to waste a minute. Until the day she died, my mother was a creative, successful businesswoman, tough mother, and loving grandmother. Though tiny, she had the strength of a giant, with more energy at seventy-seven than any two twenty-year-olds. Right up until the end, she accomplished more in one morning than most people did in a week. Her presence was a force felt by all. She was known by hundreds, each having their own personal story of how she had a positive impact on their life. She was blunt with her honesty, feelings, and thoughts, and people respected her for it. She cared about everyone she knew and their families. She loved travelling the world and cared deeply about the people in it. She embodied action, not talk; she mobilized groups and got things done. She was involved with book clubs, writing clubs, and women's groups. She took continuing education classes on a variety of topics until the end.

Her parties were magnificent, with fun, beautifully-set tables and interesting individuals, many times a group that did not know each other. She would invite those who were alone in the world to holiday dinners and make them a part of our family. At each party, she had different questions ready for her guests to motivate and provoke thought and honest engagement. Lifelong friendships formed at these parties. She was creative and loved the theater, symphony, and opera. She loved to read books and write stories. She always wanted to write a book, especially one for children.

My maternal grandmother first saw my father in the hallway outside her apartment. He was visiting a friend, and right then she decided this was who her daughter would marry. This may be a good time to mention my father's looks: Let's just say if he were standing next to Cary Grant or George Clooney, they would look like road-kill. My father had been in love with a woman, perhaps the only love of his life, but she had asthma and that was a deal breaker for my dad's mother. I'm not sure how my parents' courtship went, but I know my paternal grandmother never approved and made it very clear to my mother and grandmother. Somehow, my parents still got married.

My father was sent off to boarding school at the age of five by indifferent parents. My mother was raised in an atmosphere of fear, chaos, and unpredictability with an emotionally distant father. My mother, a woman who desperately needed the love and approval of a man, married my father, a man who survived by destroying the women who loved him. A match made in hell. My mother shared with me that she knew on her wedding night she had made a mistake. I believe my mother loved my father very much when they got married, but his indifference towards her started on that night. Were all the signs there before they married and she ignored them?

84

As all couples did in those days, they began having children right away. They were known to the outside world as a creative, funny, and happy couple. They wore it well, but the marriage quickly unraveled. Caught in the crossfire were their children, lost in a world they didn't understand, little souls whose spirits were quashed, unable to find loving comfort. There was no safety net to protect us from crashing down in a world of darkness. I was the child who stood with fists while others in the cycle were angry, or invisible. In our home behind closed doors, my parents put each other down, constantly. The children were also being put down. For me, it was whenever I asked to be seen.

My home was very loud, with everyone yelling at everyone else and putting each other down so somehow the one yelling the loudest could feel better about him or herself. Even though my parents fought constantly, I believed my father still loved and adored me. He was my daddy; he was everything to me and we were very close. I believe this put a strain on my relationship with my mother, forcing me into the role of the "other woman." It was a role I would play throughout my relationship with my father and all the women in his life—and there were a lot of women. I call this the **triangle strangle**, and this inappropriate behavior created much undue pain and havoc for me and, more importantly, for my child. I saw it as my father loving me and my thinking I was special, and it became a game where I had to win at all costs. The problem was that I didn't know I was playing a game; I thought it was what I had to do to get him to love me. It wasn't until I understood this role I was given that I was able to stop participating in this type of behavior. It felt dirty and disgusting, and I became physically ill, initially blaming myself for participating in his sick game. I didn't understand the rules or boundaries, didn't even know I was playing a game in the first place. I forgot that I was just a little girl when it started.

85

My memories of my parents as a couple are filled with scenes of fighting, belittling, and yelling at deafening levels. I often sat in the hallway outside my parents' bedroom door listening to them fight. When, one day, they brought me and one of my siblings into their room to tell us they were divorcing and Daddy was leaving, I could not understand why everyone but me was sad and crying. I thought the fighting and scariness of it all was going to end. I was relieved. I thought my mother would start seeing me and love me again. Oh, how I wished for that. I know I did not understand the outcome of the situation and was definitely not prepared for the fallout that occurred afterwards. Little did I know, it was the end of my age of innocence. I was eight.

We were one of the first families in the sixties to divorce. The marriage ended and my father ran. The father I had known and depended on was gone, just gone. He would show up sometimes for his visits. Sometimes he wouldn't. I never knew. I would sit downstairs in our lobby, or stand in our driveway waiting for him to come, always waiting. I would sit and stand, wait and wait. It was devastating when he didn't come. I did not spend much time with him even when he did show up. Usually he did so with another woman, or he would take me to some woman's house and put me in a room with her children. He had lots of women. When he didn't show up, I had to endure the angry, vile rant from my mother about how horrible he was. Story has it that he only paid child support once and never paid any alimony. He left his family as abruptly as his parents left him at boarding school.

Talk about repeating patterns!

Throughout my childhood—and well into adulthood—I felt the pain of unfulfilled expectations. I was always excited by promises. They made me feel special, like I counted. I would dream about them, fantasize about them, and wait for my dream of a promise to come true. I lived a lot of my childhood in those fantasies and dreams, and I had control over the music in the background of those dreams. It was an easier place to live.

Each time I was confronted with a broken promise, and most were broken or came with a very high emotional price tag, my world would shatter. Yet, each time a promise arose I would continue to dream, hope, wish, and fantasize. It was the wonderment of possibilities that is so simply a child's and I took those wishes and dreams with me well in to my adulthood. If, however, a promise was fulfilled, I often paid a high price in the aftermath. In moments of clarity, and I do mean moments, I would be constantly shocked and overwhelmed by how short lived those promised moments were.

After the divorce, the **abandonment** and neglect began. My father, living in his own narcissistic world, continued his journey of women, the more the better, in his ever-seeking conquest to screw women. I call it that because I believe due to his own neglect and abandonment from his mother, he lived his life screwing her through other women and somehow was paying her back for the damage she did to him. In therapeutic terms, I would call this screw the mother. Not in a sexual way. I don't think the women were about lovemaking. They were about my father not having the capacity to love, really love. I know he never learned what love was.

After my father left, I don't think I ever felt safe again. I was glad the fighting in our home between my parents was over, but my father—the loving, kind daddy I felt safe with—had disappeared. I know I was not happy. After the divorce, I never felt loved. I thought I felt loved by my father, but I was really playing the role of the woman in the middle. He came in and out of my life, with a traumatizing impact. I spent my childhood building a tough exterior, one behind which I would not have to feel the hurt and fear of being unloved. I stood with fists, not in violence, but to ward off the pain and attacks I felt all around me.

Though my parents were no longer together, the fighting and put downs did not stop. My mother used screaming as her way to communicate and always seemed to be enraged. She constantly put down my father in front of us. It was always about how much she hated him. She had good reason, but the impact of her bad-mouthing was harmful to my young spirit. She hated him until the day she died, and always let me know this. My father also had nothing nice to say about my mother, again announcing his hatred in front of his children. Their constant putting each other down pulled on my loyalties to each one. I was always put in a position to take sides, which I never could, so was torn apart. The unpredictability made me fragile and my feelings of loss were deep. As my sense that I did not matter grew, I started to feel that nobody cared, nobody saw. I was scared and drowning in my sadness without an understanding of or words to describe it.

My mother needed to work to support us. She had been a kindergarten schoolteacher at the time of the separation, but that wasn't enough to feed four mouths—and besides, she hated it. She chose another profession, a 24/7 career move that left little time for her children. When I became an adult, she told me that from the very beginning she understood her actions and the cost of them for her children. She sent us all to therapy. Whenever I had a problem with what was going on around me, my mother would shut me down and tell me to discuss it with my therapist. Therapists were raising her children. Did she feel she had no other choice? Did we children scare her with our emotional needs, so immense and fragile?

My father didn't know how to show affection because he had never been taught how. He didn't understand empathy or sympathy because he had never been shown any. He stopped growing emotionally at an age when one finds purpose in life. Consequently, he never found his own purpose and was never able to form proper attachments to those who loved him. However, he did learn that children were dispensable. Due to my father's inability to commit and love, he began cheating on my mother early in their marriage.

I was three when my younger brother was born. When she delivered him, my father was nowhere to be found. I have a vivid memory of my mother, my newborn baby brother, and me at a friend's house. My mother was holding my brother and I was sitting on another couch looking at them. My mother was in great distress. I remember feeling very sad and lonely as if it happened yesterday. I have heard that my father was out with another woman. He couldn't be bothered to participate in this occasion of a new life, his son being born. My mother suffered. Here she was with young

89

children, one a newborn, and an absent, philandering husband. I know she was overwhelmed, scared, and depressed. The more dejected and depressed she became, the harder it was for her children.

My father was constantly giving her mixed messages of love and hate. He would draw her in then spit her out. One minute he would tell her how much he loved her and couldn't imagine his life without her, and shortly after tell her he didn't really mean it, reinforcing her feelings that she was unlovable and less than worthy of him. I always think of the story my mother shared with me throughout my life about when our young family was bike riding. According to my mother, my father would ride up next to her and tell her he loved her. Seconds later he would ride up next to her and say, "I changed my mind, I don't love you." My mother was put in the **double bind**. She said it happened repeatedly that day. I can only imagine her pain and sadness over the cruelty of my father's behavior.

As the cycle of abuse repeats, I recently went through a similar experience with my father. He called me after twelve years of us not speaking. I was fifty-four, three years after my mother was killed, and well on my way in my recovery. A dear friend of his had just died and it seemed he was feeling remorseful over our split. He told me he missed me, loved me, and wanted me back in his life. He never called his children after my mother's death and did not attend her funeral, only sending us a letter. I had been attempting to reach my father since my mother died and he refused all my phone calls. My instinct was not to trust him. Our history told me so.

Yet in that moment, I was a little girl who missed and wanted her daddy in her life. That's how it works. My intuition was screaming the all-too-familiar, *danger, danger, danger!*

He told me he would call me back, as he had to deal with some issues in his life before we could reunite. I waited and waited for a call, knowing in the back of my mind I had again walked back into his madness.

Two weeks went by with no call. I summoned my tools, and instead of beating myself up for accepting him back in my life, I realized my lifelong need for my father and nurtured myself through the disappointment. When he finally called me back: "I was wrong. I don't love you or want you back in my life. I am the victim here." I admit I reacted in anger. How could I not? I screamed, expressing my disbelief that he did this to me again and I took the bait. When the call ended, I sat to quiet my inner turmoil and took deep breaths. I quickly shifted my thinking to my recovery and decided to take a different path, putting what I now know is closure to our relationship.

I am proud of the fact that I was willing to forgive and move forward. My child and I did good, so shame on him. *He lost* a kind and caring daughter. I can now move on, for I know I did everything in my power to have a relationship with my father. I have another part of my history in abuse that I can let go of. I went back in and cared for my little girl. Together we forgave and have moved on. *It's tiring!*

91

I must remind myself: Even when I have spent time with my father, he wasn't always "there." His way of dealing with and taking responsibility for his behavior was to dissociate from reality and simply leave the building. His body would still be present, but the man would go missing. **Dissociation** is a coping defense where a person disconnects from their memories, actions, thoughts, and feelings. Their sense of identity is shattered. He could be in the same room, sitting on the same couch, an uncomfortable conversation going on; his body was there, but his mind was outside. He would disappear—just emotionally go away. That way he did not have to deal or be responsible for anything.

As an adult, I truly understand my father's need to disconnect from reality. His early trauma shut him down and he never learned how to cope or take responsibility for his actions. Those years for young children when parents are supposed to create safety and security didn't exist for him. He was never nurtured. How could he pass along something he never learned to do? His parents provided no road map. Dissociation, therefore, had probably allowed him to stay alive. It was always his way of coping whenever he was asked to be an adult and take responsibility for his behavior and actions, or if anything emotional was asked of him. It happened whenever my dad was asked to feel. It was his way of life: Create the shit then leave, as I call it. One minute he was there; the next, gone. After trying to reach out to him over the years and having to deal with his behavior along with him refusing my calls, I eventually cut all ties with my father in my thirties (except his recent call). I couldn't deal with his behavior anymore. As for my behavior, I never felt my mother or siblings saw my need for my father. They were unable or unwilling to understand my sense of loss.

My mother was hanging by a thread, dealing with her own lifetime's worth of fears and further disappearing into her insecurities. She was broke—both financially and in spirit—and was left with young children to support, fragile souls dependent on an already-fractured family. She panicked. How would she, how would her family, survive? How could she raise her very lost children, who were suffering in their own spirit-crushing pain? Ultimately, two adults bowed out of their parenting roles. Two parents abandoned little spirits to fend for themselves. Both simply left their responsibility to their lost and invisible children. Gone. Here, I believe, is where my world fell apart.

I cannot speak for my siblings, for their reality is theirs to tell. This is my story and how it was for me. My mother chose to have a life at the expense of her children. I always felt like mothering got in her way. She did not have the tools to handle work, family, and her own personal life, so she made sure we got therapy to deal with the fallout of her behavior, actions, and mothering. Therapists raised her children, whose needs were enormous.

When my mother did come home, she was met by angry, yelling children who did whatever they could to get her attention. The two oldest, I being one of them, yelled the loudest. The youngest was lost in his pain. This scared my mother, and she would run away to all her endeavors in the outside world. The children were left home alone in their anger and sadness, in the damage she left behind.

I spent most of my life knowing my mother loved me, but always feeling she didn't care enough about me to be there.

When things got tough and I really needed her presence, she ran. She chose everyone and everything else except me. She couldn't connect with me in an emotional way and be there when I really needed her. It has always crushed me, and though I don't think she did any of this with intentional cruelty, my mother knew what she was doing and chose to do it anyway.

My mother was relentless with her forceful, blunt words, razor sharp and intense, which often left me on my knees in stunned silence. She had no respect for boundaries, nor regard for the impact of her actions. If questioned, she would strike back with more cruel words. She never saw the annihilation she caused, driven by her inflexible and inexhaustible obsessions and fears. Her anxiety couldn't cease, couldn't slow, couldn't calm.

My mother began her relationship with Jack when I was in my late twenties. Jack became one of two father figures I had since my father left. The first was a relationship she had with a wonderful man, who moved in with us after the divorce when I was young. I can't remember for how long. He was kind and loving to me. With Jack, there were times when we had a functional relationship, but he, too, had a side that was very abusive toward both my mother and me. The cycle continued.

What was puzzling and exasperating about all of this is that she loved, though I never understood her way of loving. Her love for me was as intense as her words. I learned at a young age of that very thin line between love and abuse. She was a wonderful woman consumed by guilt and pain over choices she made, many made from a place she felt was out of her control: a single mother with no financial support from our father. She was consumed by the fear, confusion, and drama of her life. She was driven, but sadly most of her energy was due to an inability to stop, even for a moment. She kept so busy so she wouldn't have time to think. Thinking was scary for her, dangerous even.

One day, in her early seventies, my mother admitted this to me on the phone as she was undergoing stage one breast cancer treatment. She plowed through the surgery and radiation. I believe it was during her second to last treatment of radiation when my mother got tired—once—and took a nap. I asked why I seemed to be more concerned than she was during her cancer and radiation treatments. It felt out of balance. I was thousands of miles away and it had been difficult for me not to be with her during this time. Her answer made perfect sense in its simplicity and sadness.

"If I slow down, if I stop long enough to think," she said, "I will fall apart." In a heartbeat, I got it. This was my mother. This is what drove her all these years. She could not stop. She could not think. She could not feel, for she would have fallen apart. But she did feel, did think. This revelation broke my heart: She was falling apart. I got it and understood its intensity because it was me as a child and young adult. It was me in the hole. It was me in the darkness. We were connected. If we stopped, if we thought, we would fall apart.

My mother had vision and purpose. She was a leader who never knew her power and strengths. She never understood how many friends adored her, or the impact she had on the world. She would often call me in distress because she thought this person or. that one hated her. It saddened me because it wasn't true. I believe it was her unassuming spirit, not knowing her impact, which endeared her to all. There were more than six hundred people at her funeral: standing room only.

She was complex, interesting, and strong, yet conflicted, anxious, and scared. She gave me many gifts despite all the insanity. Though she was unable to be a mother to her children, she was a role model in caring for others, caring about the world, and saying it like it is. Because of her, I have a passion for travel, the arts, music, and making the world a better place. The greatest gift she ever gave me was to appreciate the differences in color and culture. She taught me to be curious, to want to learn about the world and embrace its diversity. She got that gift from her mother, another pioneer who was way ahead of her time. I am forever grateful to my mother and grandmother, both of whom had power in ways I could never comprehend. It was magic and madness.

At the end of my mother's life, I know the abuse beat her down. I saw it, watched it, and I begged her to change it. She wouldn't, perhaps couldn't. She began to take a look at her life and the players in it. Her feelings and thoughts were growing louder and louder, beginning to take over the pace of her running. I believe she was able to discuss some of these fears with a woman's group she belonged to. There were certain friends with whom she began to talk about her life. She was slowly telling her secrets. Her journey out may have been beginning, yet she was still unable to take the action to save herself. Her anxiety over her situation was inconsolable, and it broke my heart to watch. And, though I tried, I knew there was nothing I could do to rescue her.

I mentioned the following terms: dissociation, double bind, and triangle strangle. These are terms I began to use in my twenties to understand my parents' and my reactions to what was going on. My personal dissociative tendency is to feel disconnected from myself and from what is going on around me in order to survive the abuse when it escalates. It often has felt like an out-of-body experience, and since my world was so riddled with double binds and mixed messages, I had constant trouble connecting to its unpredictability. These contradictions I received baffled my senses so I didn't know what was what. I began to split off parts of the trauma from my awareness and consciousness, minimizing the events so I could keep moving forward, rewriting my memories so they wouldn't overwhelm, making the intolerable tolerable. It was a no-win situation for me, always. Combine that with my father setting me up in a triangle with all the women in his life, including my mother, and you get what I refer to as my **crazy-making reality**.

I have lived with abuse my whole life. I didn't always know it was abusive because I had nothing with which to compare my situation. As I grew, I knew. I knew that being raged at, belittled, abandoned, invalidated, and made to feel worthless and stupid was not right. I knew my spirit and ability to flourish were being crushed. The abuse let me know I was in trouble at an early age, but without the language and life tools to change this for myself, I fell apart internally and lived that way through most of my life. From the outside, however, things may have looked normal.

Again, the cycle of abuse repeats itself from generation to generation if not stopped. It also cycles within a relationship from abusive incident to calm and back. If your children are growing up in abuse, the damage is done. Don't kid yourself. They are watching your poor coping and adaptive skills and learning that abuse is the norm. Fathers show their children how women are treated, and mothers how to treat men. If you give children the message that abuse is normal, that it is somehow okay, many grow up to abuse or be abused. However, those who avoid abusive relationships as adults are still likely to suffer from growing up in turmoil.

Teens and young adults may get pregnant with the wish for someone to unconditionally love them. The rationale behind this is quite obviously flawed. Another tendency is to rush into committed relationships to escape their homes and ignore or minimize any incompatibility with their partners, which places them in subordinate roles either consciously or unconsciously. All these poor decisions are rooted in feelings of being unloved and desperate to feel counted. The scenarios are many, and most with disastrous results, only repeating the cycle into each new generation.

I never married, nor had children because I was so afraid I would not be an emotionally connected parent and would repeat the cycle of abuse. While I'm grateful for the impossibility of this now, the loss due to my internalized abuse is immeasurable because I always wanted to be a mommy and have a family. The reasoning behind my decision is not the answer. Choosing not to marry or have children is a right, and there is nothing wrong with this choice if it is how you feel. To do this out of fear leaves a lot of holes in the spirit. I'm not sure it was a conscious choice, but it was a choice. I'd like others to learn from my mistakes

CHAPTER FOUR
ME AS THE COMMON DENOMINATOR

I believe intuition is one of the best strengths each human possesses. We hear it all the time, yet are so willing to ignore it unless we truly tap into its purpose and exactness.

Me as the Common Denominator

"No one can make you feel inferior without your consent."
~ Eleanor Roosevelt ~

Throughout my past attempts to leave the abusive circle, my mother would have meltdowns, devastated by the thought of us breaking apart. As sick as our dynamics were, keeping the family together was the most important thing to her. It's what kept her glued. For the longest time, I stayed because of this. Even when I explained my need to get away from the cycle, she never seemed to understand. She always minimized the abuse and the effect it was having on me. It never occurred to her that what I was telling her was valid, or she knew and just couldn't deal with the truth. I didn't choose abuse, but I chose my mother and that kept me stuck in its debilitating cycle. And that choice to stay, like the choice to not have children, was made out of fear. I had no self-esteem and no internal belief that I could survive in a world where I didn't understand the rules of life.

In my late forties, during a time of intense full-time growth, I decided the only way I could truly heal was to move away from my family and leave the town where I grew up. It was something I had wanted to do forever and finally felt strong enough to take my leap of faith. My deciding factor to move was an incident with my mother: I had been the associate director of a social work department at a non-profit organization, where I worked for more than twelve years. Due to my mother's anxiety, if she could not reach me on the phone, she was prone to calling the director of my department, and at times the executive director of the agency, in a panic over where I was. I was mortified when

101

this would happen, yet could not get her to understand how inappropriate her actions were. Not once did it occur to her how this reflected on my job and professionalism. Desperate for a break from the chaos, during a week where she was calling non-stop, I decided not to answer her phone calls for a couple of days.

Around day three of not answering, I was at home spending a quiet evening. At ten-thirty that night, there was a loud banging on my door. When I answered, there stood my mother. As I peeked out into the hallway, Jack was leaning against the wall as if hiding. He looked at me and mouthed the words, "I have nothing to do with this." My mother was enraged, spewing how she had thought I was dead and admonishing me for not answering her calls. I was responsible for the turmoil of her anxieties.

All the **triggers** of my lifetime were pulled in that moment. My want for peace and a respite from all the mayhem ignored once again, my needs invisible. As my mother went on and on, I wondered how she was able to get to my front door. I lived in a high-rise building with security and a twenty-four hour doorman. No one was allowed to enter the building without the tenant being called and buzzing the person in. If the doorperson let someone in, his job was on the line. How did my mother get past the security? As calm as I could remain, I stood in the doorway as my mother exploded. I don't even remember how long she stayed. Dump, spew, rage. And then she was gone, always. Create the shit then leave.

I went down to the lobby to see what had happened. I was told my mother got angry with the doorman, refused to let him call me, and barged through the front door when someone came out. The doorman was upset and scared he would be fired. I assured him I would go to the office the next morning on his behalf, forever fixing what is not mine. As I entered my apartment after all this, I knew if I didn't leave, I would die.

I gave notice shortly after this incident and held tightly to Anaïs Nin's poem, ready to take the risk, ready to blossom. I decided to take a year off, move away, and create a new normal. Four months later, I packed up my car, locked my front door, and left for the mountains, where I'd wanted to live my whole life.

But first, half a decade earlier, when I was forty-three years old, I was in a bicycle accident. I believe it was the beginning of real change for me, the first time that I said I'd had enough and meant it. This accident was the catalyst for me deciding to change my reality, the period I decided to move out of the darkness. I became **sick and tired of being sick and tired**, or at least finally realized this to be true. It was my first conscious rock bottom, and the landing was inhospitable. There was no one there to take my order: *Rocks, no salt.*

I believe intuition is one of the best strengths each human possesses. We hear it all the time, yet are so willing to ignore it unless we truly tap into its purpose and exactness. Some just believe in it and let it guide them. My intuition has been strong and ever-present since I was a small child, though my ability to disregard it was even stronger. Whenever I would have a premonition, my family would either ignore me, laugh, or put me down for being stupid. I silenced my intuition, but always had it. That is how it worked for me until my accident.

I was going to a two-day bike event. I had decided to do an AIDS ride the following summer and this was going to be my first long training ride towards that goal. Days before I left, I began to have bad feelings about the trip. Everything inside me was telling me not to go. Actually it was screaming for me not to go. The emotion felt so strong that I shared my feelings with my boss. He told me I should not go. I thought I had to. I was meeting friends, had agreed to split hotel costs with them, and I didn't want to disappoint anyone, an ongoing theme for me. This conversation with my boss went on all week. Same thing the day I left. The intuition screaming: *Don't go, don't go, don't go.* Guess what? I went. That's how my intuition worked for me. I heard it loud and clear then snubbed it.

The morning of the first day, my friends and I were preparing for the ride. We were in a school parking lot dressing, packing, and making sure tire pressure was good before making our way to the start point. We were late, and most riders were already well on their way. On the way to the start, there was a speed bump in the road. Earlier that morning it had been marked by yellow tape. There was also a sign, mostly hidden behind a tree, indicating the bump. The yellow tape had worn off due to so many riders traveling over it, and I did not see the sign. Or the bump. I was not going fast and did not even have my helmet on yet since we had not officially started the ride.

I hit the bump and lost control. My foot got caught in my pedal clip and I could not regain my balance or get my foot out to stop the fall. The last thing I remember was falling through the air and thinking, "Oh, shit!" What I don't remember was hitting the ground.

When I came to, I felt fine. I didn't even know I had passed out. As I tried to get up, I lost my breath and went back

104

into unconsciousness. I came to a second time, tried to get up and again lost consciousness. The third time, I opened my eyes to a doctor standing over me telling me not to move.

He said I had broken my clavicle and that it was sticking out. That seemed ridiculous to me. I felt fine and just wanted to get up and start my ride. An ambulance showed up. I couldn't understand why I needed an ambulance. The paramedics began to immobilize my neck and body to a board, putting tape over my forehead to secure me down. I thought that too was ridiculous. I was in no pain and refused to believe I had broken a bone. I had been an athlete my whole life. Tough sports like hockey—both ice and field—mountain climbing, and marathon running, and now I was in training for the AIDS ride. Aside from the typical sprains and bruises, I had never been injured, never broken anything. Good "Grade A" calcium rich bones: that was me.

The paramedic wanted to give me a shot for the pain. I told him I wasn't in any and refused. He wanted to start a morphine drip. I wasn't interested. I was tough. I could handle it. My whole life had prepared me for this moment. It never occurred to me that I was in shock. It never occurred to me that my bone was really broken. This had to be a conspiracy. They were all lying. I couldn't be vulnerable; I didn't know how.

They got me to the emergency room and asked about my pain. I hung tough; I wasn't in any. They didn't even put me in a room, just stuck me against a wall right in the emergency room with all the frenzy mulling around me. As I lay there, I again felt invisible. Every once in a while, a nurse would come up to ask me how I was. I was fine. I was tough. My friend came in and out of the ER to see me. He kept telling me I should call my mother to let her know what happened. I would not call her. I didn't want to deal with her anger and knew I would disappear into her anxieties. She was the last person I wanted by my side.

105

After what seemed like hours of lying against a wall with no pain medication, being the perfect little patient and not causing any trouble, things began to shift. My shock was wearing off, as was my ability to portray toughness, a defense I had learned in order to survive. *I'll be tough so no one can hurt me.* And then it happened. They wheeled a woman into the ER and I heard them say she had broken her clavicle. They rushed her right into a room, where doctors and nurses swarmed her. *Her* injury was serious. I broke down. The pain I felt was horrendous and shot straight through my whole body with lightning speed, engulfing and consuming me.

They rushed this woman to the X-ray room. After all, she had a broken clavicle and that was a serious break. Hey, what about me? I'd been there for hours, and other than the occasional nurse checking on me, nothing had progressed. Wasn't I told I had a broken clavicle? Why wasn't mine as important as this other woman's? Why was I always invisible? There I lay, with **me as the common denominator** in my own story.

I lost it. I became indignant, angry, and scared. It wasn't until I broke down crying that anyone noticed. The excruciating pain and fear bore through my senses. I was broken, literally and figuratively. After that, the nurse wheeled me toward the X-ray room. I was behind the woman who had come in minutes ago to my hours. I wailed to the nurse. Why she was ahead of me if we had the same break? Why had I been ignored in the ER? It was so unfair; how could they do this to me? I fell into a conscious darkness as the woman was wheeled into the room. I was internally enraged and externally lost, and by the time I made it into the X-ray room, I was a wreck. They hoisted me from the stretcher to the X-ray table like a slab of raw meat. The pain shot straight through my eyeballs. The X-rays came back confirming a broken clavicle, plus two broken ribs and a broken scapula. And let's not forget the hit my head took on the pavement. The other woman only had a broken clavicle.

"I won."

After being X-rayed, they brought me back to the ER, only this time I was wheeled into a room. I was still shaken and in a tremendous amount of pain as the medical team began to work on me. I was still in my tight bike clothes and sweatshirt. They started to remove my sweatshirt by lifting my arms over my head, a solution I can't comprehend how a room of medical staff would have considered viable.

That was it for me. I was done, this time literally. The pain spiked through my body and I was sent to a different stratosphere. I felt myself falling fast. All of a sudden, I was looking down at myself and knew I was dying. I had left my body and was no longer in pain. I couldn't believe it. I was stunned. But more than anything, I was livid. I wasn't ready to die. How could this be happening?

I watched them rip apart my clothes and attach wires all over my body. "We're losing her," I heard them say, frantically hooking my body up to machines. Was I dead? I couldn't be; this wasn't happening. I don't know how long I stayed in this suspended state. Furious, I think it was sheer will that reconnected me with my body. I didn't want to dive back into it, into all the pain, but that's what I did. And it seemed that as quickly as I left my body, I came back. After, I remember wondering: *Where were the pictures of my family? Where was the white light?* I've heard wonderful stories from people who have had near death experiences of the calm peace and that light. I had none of that.

I was closely monitored in the hospital that night on a morphine drip. While I continued to act tough on the outside, cracking jokes and pretending to be fine, I was really quite vulnerable. The fact that I had to make some drastic changes in my life became clear. I looked up to the ceiling for my direct line to God. I had never really thought much about God before that moment, only that I didn't believe there was one. So I looked up to the ceiling to my new buddy and said: *Okay, you have my complete attention. What? What do you want from me? What do you want me to do? Talk to me. Tell me. Give me the rules and the steps. Some direction on how to do this would be helpful. I know you have been giving me signs all week and I once again ignored them. So here I am. I'm paying attention. What am I supposed to learn from this?*

When God didn't answer, I knew it was up to me to figure out what I needed to do. What I *did* realize in that moment were all the signs around me. Perhaps the gift from God was having been awakened from a life of conscious unconsciousness, of ignoring to the signs. Now that I knew what was happening to me and why, I could no longer go back to my unconscious state. I had to give up my denial, stop minimizing my life situation, and deal. After all, there I was, lying in that bed. I couldn't move and I couldn't run away. I was stuck with me right up in my own face. God's pretty smart.

This was the beginning of my journey towards healing, both psychologically and now physically. If I didn't take it,

I knew I would die emotionally. And there I lay, with me as the common denominator. That spiritual moment was short-lived as the reality hit that I had to call my mother, a mother who became angry when I got sick or hurt, sunk in. I dreaded calling her, but had no choice. I was six hours away from home with my car. I wanted to go home and needed someone to drive.

My mother flew down the next day to get me. I wanted a loving hug, my hair stroked and to be assured that everything would be okay. What I got was tightly woven concern and frigidity, all wrapped up in a little package of imposition. This is how she loved.

But she did love.

We spent the night at a hotel before driving home. I asked her to help wash my hair and clean my body. So disgusted, she could barely touch me. When she did, it was none too gentle. She spent the remainder of the night on the phone, her lifeline to work. I was invisible to her yet again. Comments or requests for attention were met with anger. This was always her method: Aren't you *grateful* that I'm here? Does it *look* like I have time to be connected to you?

The next morning, I was trying to figure out how to position my body into my Ford Explorer and make it through a six hour drive. I took pillows from the hotel to cushion myself. I was heavily medicated, which did nothing for the pain that was still radiating through my whole being. My mother insisted that I stay awake the whole ride home—who knows why, other than her omnipresent anxiety and anger. I was drugged, exhausted, and in pain. While heading back, it occurred to me that I could not go home and take care of myself. I lived alone. I couldn't go to the bathroom. My beloved king-sized bed was dangerously high. I was helpless. Oh, and I wasn't allowed to sleep. The ride home sucked.

My desperation left me no choice but to go to my mother's. Instead of taking me to her house, my mother went straight to a hospital where a very renowned doctor was going to take a look at my injuries, or at least I assumed that was what he was going to do. My mother always knew the best, or knew somebody who knew somebody who was the best. I entered his office with my mother in tow. She insisted—forget that I was forty-three and asked her not to. I didn't want her there. I didn't want my meeting with the doctor to become about her anxiety. I didn't want to disappear. She ignored my request and followed me straight into the exam room. I instantly reverted to the flippant, stands-with-fists mentality of childhood. It's how I survived being with my mother.

They took X-rays, spoke about my clavicle and recovery. I asked about all my other broken bones. Didn't they want X-rays of them? Didn't they want to talk about healing the rest of my body? The doctor would not hear me. I couldn't believe it. He only wanted to talk about my clavicle. I was cut off from discussing the rest. My mother was disruptive and intrusive as always. I wanted to get up and walk out, but couldn't. I was hurt and defenseless. A kind of straightjacket sling held my clavicle in place, and the doctor showed my mother how to wrap it around my body. I was terrified of my mother's touch and I went into a zombie-like survival mode.

110

Not only had my own façade undermined the purity of my life experiences and prevented true vulnerability, but it had now almost killed me. Who was my authentic self? I wasn't sure yet, but I knew she needed a loving, nurturing guide. Why couldn't I believe I was worth that or allow myself to have it? Why couldn't my mother give that to me? But these questions weren't the most pressing matter, as I was preoccupied preparing for the inevitable, returning to my mother's home and all that would entail. Having to go to a place where my psyche was under constant attack was frightening, but I had no choice. I was too tired to fight. I had to prepare myself for the challenge of recovery. Hell, what was one more challenge in an already broken self? Only this time, the fractures were also physical. Finally, we got to her house.

My mother woke me early every morning to make sure I was alive. Problem was, I had usually just fallen asleep because it took most of the night to find comfortable positions, of which there were none. For the first week, I had to sleep sitting up due to my broken ribs. Exhaustion would finally take over and I would sleep, usually a couple of hours before my mother would wake me. As soon as she did and saw I was breathing, she would run out of the house. Every morning, the same thing. I would be left to my pain and unable to fall back asleep.

She was so curt with me; tenderness was non-existent. Helping me to the bathroom, bathing me, and putting my body sling on were all exercises in futility. Her anger, anxiety, and inability to help were always in the forefront. Jack was there at night, after work, quiet and out of the way. I don't blame him.

The following weekend, my two-year-old nephew became very ill. My sister-in-law, who was pregnant with my niece, called my mother in a panic. My mother rushed up to my room and told me we were leaving to go to an emergency room forty-five minutes away. Still in extreme pain, moving was a real challenge. I had to dress, make it down three flights of steep stairs, and climb up into the SUV of my very impatient and dismissive mother. On the drive, I inquired about my brother and why he was not rushing to the hospital to be with his sick son and pregnant wife. I got no answer.

We arrived at the emergency room to find a very sick little boy and a very scared mother. When I asked where my brother was, my sister-in-law said he was not to be called or disturbed during his retreat, a retreat where he was learning how to become a better human being, father, and husband. It was okay to drag me quite a distance to be with my sick nephew, yet not okay to call his father to come home? I was shocked. I endured yet another very long, uncomfortable day in an emergency room. Don't get me wrong. I adore my nephew, one of the loves of my life and favorite humans on the planet, with every pore of my being. I was very concerned. My frustrations weren't about him.

My nephew ended up being okay. They gave him a spinal tap, his fever broke, and by the time we got him home, he looked as good as new. Babies are so resilient. But I was a wreck. I had a horrible argument on the phone with my brother. Where the hell was he? He told me the group where he was becoming enlightened would not let him leave, that they made him choose between his family and the weekend. I believe he was stuck with his own ghosts. How's that for enlightenment? He didn't return home until later that evening, and by that time, his son was fine.

The day reminded me of when that same brother was about six years old and lost his grip of the uneven bars at school. He fell right on his head. My mother and I rushed to the hospital. I remember how sick my brother was and the doctors not knowing how he would do. I also remember my father yelling at my mother when she called him: "You exaggerate everything. He'll be fine." My father did not come to the hospital. Mostly, I remember my mother's tears and worries. They finally gave my brother a spinal tap and he was okay. My father showed up the next day saying to my mother, "See?"

I still have visions of my brother playing in his hospital bed that morning like nothing ever happened. I could not understand him going through the experience of not having his father show up to an emergency room when he was severely hurt and then turning around and doing the same to his son.

Again, notice the patterns.

My mother was getting ready to go to Cuba and my being hurt was an inconvenience. My brother and sister-in-law invited me to stay with them once my mother left, but I felt that was not a safe plan. My nephew was only two years old at the time and I didn't think I could handle being around such a small, active child. My sister-in-law was pregnant and I felt like my presence would only be an intrusion. I had to figure out my alternatives. The trip was approaching fast.

As the day came for me to leave my mother's, I called all my friends to see if they could help me move my stuff home. I was going to figure out how to care for myself when I got there. Not one friend could help me, no one. I was devastated. I felt I was always there to help my friends with time, listening, and offering guidance if needed.

It was my life as of **co-dependency**, always giving myself to others and, in that moment for example, feeling righteous indignation when someone would not give back to me. It didn't occur to me that I had waited until the last moment to ask for help, or that it was a workday for all my friends.

This felt familiar: I had no friends to turn to *in my time of need*, an empty feeling at its best. I was in my mother's living room, despondent. It was becoming very clear to me I was in trouble and needed help. I would not be able to take care of myself and I was not ready to return home. I was alone again, me as the common denominator.

My mother was packing. She stormed downstairs into the kitchen and I followed. She was on the phone with Jack about how she couldn't leave me alone. She was talking about canceling the trip. I was relieved. She hung up the phone, looked at me and said, "I will not stay unless you ask me." I was shocked. I didn't understand, as usual, what she was asking of me. I was her daughter, broken, in pain, and now in a state of disbelief. Why did I have to *ask* her to stay? Why couldn't she just stay because she

114

was my mother and it was the right thing to do? Why was she always so angry with me?

I asked her why she was doing this to me, why she couldn't just stay because it was the loving thing to do. She ignored me and again stated forcefully that she would not cancel her trip unless I asked her to stay. What I again heard was that, unless I begged her to stay, she would leave, abandon me and not look back. I was now more than stunned: I was spiritually broken as well, crushed. My mother, who had chosen everything and anything over parenting, had the opportunity to be a real mother—to take care of her broken daughter, to love me unconditionally. She was unmovable in her request. If I did not ask her to stay, if I did not let her know how much I needed her, if I did not beg, she would leave for Cuba. Talk about triggers! Asking and begging her to stay in my broken state cost me, and it was high.

It was rare that my mother freely gave me any positive attention. There was always a cost to being loved by her. I had no choice but to ask her to not leave for Cuba. The price I paid for asking still haunts me to this day. I felt invisible. The emotional pain was competing with my physical pain, and I could not breathe. I thought I would die. I did die a little, died a little each time my mother did this to me. I asked and she stayed. I paid the price for being loved.

I don't know why my mother did this. I often wonder if she ever noticed my pain, and even though I believed she loved, I never felt loved the way I've always dreamt it, the kind of love with flutes in the background, the kind filled with sweetness, warmth, kisses, and hugs, the kind of love that makes you feel counted and whole. I had never felt that kind of love from my mother, love that doesn't hurt. Did she hate me? At times, I think she did. Was I an intrusion on her life? Most of my growing up I certainly seemed to be. I certainly was after my accident. How dare I ask her to be a mother? Sadly, I have always felt that way.

During this time, numerous incidents at my mother's house continued to break my spirit. The heavy medication made my body numb, but it did not disguise the pain, only made me too stoned to do anything about it. Everything was an ordeal: going to the bathroom, finding a position to sleep, walking, moving, all done with extreme caution and care. Bathing and washing my very long hair was a grueling task. I mostly managed on my own, but one day was in so much pain I could not wash myself, so asked my mother to help. She was on the phone and angry at the disruption. She came into the bathroom, took a cloth and vigorously began to wash me, increasing my pain level with her roughness. She was grossed out. I was grossing her out. She could not bathe me. She could barely touch me, but she did yell at me for asking to be loved and taken care of.

The last time I asked for her help with bathing sent me over the edge. I always placed a towel on the side of the tub so it was easy to reach. One day when I was done bathing, I noticed the towel was not there. My mother, in her obsessive need for neatness, had come in and hung it up. I called for my mother and asked her to give me the towel. She was again on the phone and angry that I was interrupting her always-very-important call. When she came in, she unplugged the water, which was now

116

getting cold, and stormed out of the bathroom, the towel still hanging on its hook. I shivered as the water drained from the tub, pleading for her to come back to give it to me. She again burst into the bathroom, took the towel from the hook and threw it at me. As it landed on my head, she stormed out again.

Her behavior made me feel valueless, hated, like one big intrusion—but most of all, I felt unloved.

After my bike accident and subsequent time with my mother, I stopped trying to make sense of my family's behavior. I couldn't understand or continue to live in such a destructive pattern. I realized I had wasted a lifetime of energy trying to get something that would never materialize. My mother was unable to be anything but harsh, critical, and anxious with me. She was never capable of being the kind of mother who was soft and gentle. I couldn't waste any more time looking to parents who could not love me. This I knew: I am loveable; I am worth it. This would be my journey.

Leading up to the accident, everything in my life was telling me I had to slow down. Every ounce of intuition was there, but I chose to ignore it. I needed to stop, but refused. It was similar to my mother's need to constantly move at warped speed. Cycles repeat and we are taught by what we see.

If there is one, was this God's way of making me stop? Was the choice taken away from me? There I was, stopped in an instant, immobile in my broken body. In a split second, my life changed and I was confronted with myself. I could no

117

longer ignore what seemed like my own hand gripping my face and obstructing my vision. I had no choice but to take a look at what my life had become. *I was the common denominator.*

I had to make drastic changes for my own survival. How do I access what is deep inside me? How do I find my true authentic self: the kind, smart, strong person I am? How do I shed the façade that has enabled my survival? How do I not react in a way that sounds like my mother's rage when I am uncomfortable or being confronted? How do I tackle the pain, sadness, and depression that have been my life companions? How do I take the steps needed to reprogram the loud, critical voice in my head, my internal tape? How do I begin to restructure, taking away the old and replacing it with the new?

The one thing I did know I needed to learn was how to breathe. A simple thing, really, when you think about it: breath. I'd been holding mine for so long. I needed to breathe—in and out, in and out—and I needed to slow down to take these breaths. Breathing keeps us alive; no wonder I had felt dead for so long. So that's where I'd start: I would learn how to breathe long, deep breaths filled with oxygen—long, deep breaths that would replenish life.

When I realized the past could not change my situation, that the abusers could not make it better, my journey to health, healing, and freedom began. I realized the past cannot rewrite my history, nor can it change the people in it. The past cannot even understand what my struggles were and are. After this ah-ha moment, I had to come up with how I was going to start my journey towards a life without abuse. While I embraced this, I had to understand what verbal and emotional abuse was *for me* in order to change my thinking and behavior. Even as a therapist who understood this for my clients, I had to internally accept what was and learn from my heart, not my intellect. I had to give the responsibility of abuse to the abusers.

I spent a lifetime feeling unable to change my abusive surroundings and so had remained in this fearful and helpless place. I wanted to fix the abuse and had attempted everything I knew. Exasperation kept me stuck. I now know I couldn't fix anything. If the players in the abusive cycle do not wish to alter their behavior or believe it is abusive, change is impossible. Staying in the cycle kept me in a fearful stance and I remained stagnant and helpless. The reality is no matter how much we may love an abusive person, we cannot fix his or her problems. My conscious understanding of this and need for change began after my bicycle accident. When I got to this realization, I was about 555 into my 999 years of therapy. After those 555 years and becoming a therapist myself, it was time. But I still had a long journey ahead of me. I didn't, after all, reclaim my voice until my mother's death. Only 444 years to go.

Breathe, just breathe.

The reality is no matter how much we may love an abusive person, we cannot fix his or her problems.

CHAPTER FIVE
PUTTING BANDAGES ON MY OWN KNEES

When I realized I was still so "tight in the bud," I had to face my fears head-on to redefine myself and carve a new path. Living a life of conscious awareness became my goal.

PUTTING BANDAGES ON MY OWN KNEES

There came a point when I had to accept that their disinterest wasn't personal. It was healthier, and more practical, and certainly more comfortable all around. What was the point of breaking my heart over it when they wouldn't have noticed? Or if they had, it would have baffled them. They're not bad people, just careless parents. I am who I am because they were who they were. That's enough for me.
~Nora Roberts~

Traumatic events have happened repeatedly throughout my life. The abuse came from all around, from many different people, and has always shattered me. It was never predictable, even if I knew a verbal or physical blow was coming. I have been profoundly affected by what happened to me as a child. It has deeply touched every aspect of my being. I always felt that no one could help me, that I was all alone and drowning without the vocabulary to describe my reality to outsiders. I was quite young when the abuse began, and didn't have the sophistication to understand or explain what was happening.

I spent my childhood and the majority of my adult life stuck in a sanctimonious, self-righteous, defiant mindset. *It's not fair,* I thought. *The work is too hard, and I don't know how to fix this.* I gave away my power to change things for myself, too afraid to define what changes needed to be made, the skills I'd need to learn to make those changes, or even what those changes would look like. I was stuck in the fear of letting go, and of the unknown. I didn't know how to unclench the fists I had been standing with for so long. They were my protection.

Accepting what was and letting go was difficult, so I put the blame on everyone but myself. That way I didn't have to take responsibility for what happened and therefore didn't have to work toward change. My parents should have been the ones to work at undoing the damage. I didn't create it or cause it, so why should I have to be responsible? It wasn't fair and I didn't ask to be born.

It all sounded something like, "You big poopy heads."

That was immaturity at its best, immaturity in adulthood. This attitude created a grown-up kid who didn't understand rules or boundaries and couldn't deal with the fragile internal structure of an abused child. One day, a guest on Oprah read the above quote, from Roberts' book "Face the Fire," which had a profound impact on me. The words stopped me in my tracks. Their simplicity and dead-on accuracy perfectly explained my childhood and the parenting I received. In fact, **"That's enough for me"** is precisely what I had spent most of my adult life struggling with.

I was at a crossroads where my child and adult were colliding. When I could no longer blame my adult situation on my childhood abuse, nor on the abuse I was still enduring, I began to come to terms with my situation and figure out how to deal with my child's emotional stance. Even though I hadn't seen any white light, my bicycle accident had given me a huge light-bulb moment. Through my professional education, my own lifetime of therapy, and this accident, I understood what I needed to do: I had to reach for my little girl. But how?

When I realized I was still so "tight in the bud," I had to face my fears head-on to redefine myself and carve a new path. Living a life of conscious awareness became my goal. The work became to understand my childhood stance and remind myself that although it was not my fault, it was now my responsibility to put it behind me and move forward. *How the hell do I do that?* I didn't have a clue, nor did I have a role model to look to. But I was finding my awareness. I was growing up.?

One of my first steps was to tap into my fantasy world, which was huge, because—in my youth especially—it was better to live there than in reality. As a child, I hated mornings and the chaotic, dramatic messes they brought with them. Each day, I would wake up feeling disconnected and confused to an angry, anxious mother flicking my bedroom light on and off, screaming at me to wake up. Growing up in an apartment with little natural light only added to the darkness I felt inside. No matter what time of day it was, our apartment was always gloomy and scary. It was filled with the ghosts of abuse as well as the ghosts of a child's imagination amid all the black. At night, I would lie in my bed and carefully position my body. I could not have any part of any limb hanging over the side, so sure the monsters hiding beneath the bed would pull me under and I would disappear. I also had a fear that every time I sat on the toilet, the monsters would reach up through the toilet and suck me down. The fears children normally have were intensified by the uncertainty of abuse.

My imagination has always had a loud presence. Usually, it was a place where I made the rules and decided what would

125

happen. When I was young, I made up a story that I was from the planet Zot, named after a candy I loved (cherry my favorite flavor.) My mother was Zeka and my father was Zeus. They were wonderful and loving. My parents on Zot could fix all my problems, while mine on Earth could not.

Another favorite childhood fantasy that followed me into adulthood sounded something like this (cue music): *It has strong arms that wrap around me, holding me, caressing my hair, rocking me. It says gentle, loving words of encouragement and I am safe. There are violins in the background, maybe Beethoven or Bach. The music fills the air and soothes my soul. From this comfortable place, I am empowered to dig deep and access the pain and sadness. I am given loving permission to let go and release. I cry until exhaustion, until I am spent. It is cathartic and healing. It cleanses my spirit. It releases all the misery. I let go. I heal.*

Maybe I have seen too many movies, but a girl can dream, can't she? After these fantasies, I would write my acceptance speech for my Academy Award. *And I'd like to thank... just me.*

The fantasies of children often far outweigh reality because their developing minds are imaginative and boundless. My own reveries were very strong, but could be also be as dark and frightening. However, as I reached inward for my child, I realized these powerful daydreams could also guide me in the creation of beautiful visions of how I wanted my life to be, my new normal. I had been doing this since I was a young child, and now the next step, the focal point, was to determine how to incorporate them. How do I provide this for myself, heal, and move on? How do I become aware so I can make conscious change? I couldn't, of course, move to Zot, but I *did* move to the mountains. I *could* surround myself with wonderful, loving people. I *can* give myself permission to access my pain and let go.

As I began to hold my child, I thanked her for protecting me and validated everything she went through. I let her know her job was done; we didn't need to live in the fear and anxiety anymore. I put her into our big comfy bed to let her rest. I curled up with her, stroked her hair, and as we wrapped our arms around each other and sighed, we drifted off to sleep. It was the first of many amazing moments my child and I would have in our process of becoming one. I slowly started becoming an adult and began to believe we really *could* live without all the noise. When I got to this point, I can remember clearly thinking I would be okay without knowing exactly what to do in each step of this process. I was certain we were on our way.

During this process, I had to constantly notice my stance and unclench those fists to shift the repetitive, critical soundtrack of my existence to something more spiritually nourishing. My soul was starving. I had to be conscious of what I was hungry for as well as what would give me heartburn. I had to understand that even though I will never forget, and—in the case of some—may never forgive, at some point I needed to move on, to search for and start focusing on the good. My life, after all, wasn't working, nor were any of my relationships. I kept coming back to the same place over and over again with no change in my attitude, life, or

127

behavior. The outcome of abuse always remained the same, no matter how much I imagined the next time would be different.

Growing up in chaos and uncertainty takes a toll, a lifetime toll. Children begin to accept this type of behavior, and even if they are aware it is not okay, they are learning tools of survival as well as how to treat others. They see and hear everything, whether right or wrong, and will blame themselves for the problems. The work to recover, understand, and attempt to fill the holes is excruciating, especially with so many residual survival defenses to sift through. Thinking becomes distorted in order to make it through each day, and a damaged ego blocks the ability to self-observe and self-love. Self-worth becomes a lost goal, a concept hidden behind the pain in accessing those damaging feelings and their causes.

When we are infants, even in the womb, we innately depend on others for our very survival. When we enter into the world, our unconscious expectation is to have all our needs met: warmth, feeding, cooing, kisses, clean diapers, and soft, kind words. Our unconscious expectation is love. As we grow, we depend on these things continuing and being age appropriate so we can thrive. If that does not happen, we quickly move into survival mode. When abuse occurs before a child is verbal, or is verbally immature, it is extremely difficult if not impossible for the child to describe feelings and experiences surrounding the abuse.

In some families, older siblings may be grooming the younger ones for survival, or giving them up as the new scapegoat and target of the abuse. Others yet may give themselves up as the target of the violence in order to keep their siblings safe. All of these survival skills are methods for enduring the madness of one's family system. You can have a resilient child, a withdrawn child, and an angry child in the same family. All are experiencing the same thing, but dealing with the fallout in very different ways. The abused adult may be so beaten down that s/he does not have the ability to keep the children safe. Others become fierce, like a lioness, in protecting their children. Through it all, kids absorb the devastation.

Each of my siblings manifested what was going on around us differently. Everyone's internal structure and capacity for survival varied. As a child, I was angry and unable to verbalize, though felt I was screaming it out to empty ears. And boy, could I scream. Due to never being heard, I was never able to conjure the verbal skills to explain how I felt. The lack of guidance for me in finding my voice stunted my development and growth. It seemed that every time I attempted to explain how I was feeling, I was cut off or ignored. No one talked about what was happening. We just endured. When therapists would ask me to describe what I was feeling, I couldn't. I didn't know how. Besides, I wasn't going to tell them anything. Not knowing I had any to keep, my secrets grew larger and larger.

Without the language to discuss my problems, I acted out. Unconsciously, without understanding why, I did whatever I could to get my parents' attention. In my attempts to be heard, I would have constant conniption fits: loud, dramatic, angry, and always frightening. I was that child in the grocery store who everyone looked at. I would get so distressed and enraged I would pass out: literally pass out cold, faint dead away. My spirit would fade to black. I would pass out anywhere: in the middle of restaurants, for example, and was so scared every time I would. People seemed embarrassed by this, especially friends if I was with them when it happened. I never got comfort, and was left alone to deal with my fears and lack of understanding about what had happened. My parents, so distracted by their own turmoil and need to survive, threw little children to the side.

In high school, I started using drugs and drinking alcohol to keep me numb. I merely existed. I often wondered how I made it to school, or how I learned anything when I was there. At school, my head would be filled with the noise and the darkness. Though I was smart, learning was difficult. My body, both emotionally and chemically, was always reacting to the abuse. As I got older, I knew what was going on in my family was abusive. My intellect knew something was wrong, yet the way I internally manifested what was coming at me was unhealthy. It was my PTS reaction responding to the volatile nature of the abuse, and trying to fight off the cruelty of its intent. It destroyed, belittled, and tore me down. Passing out as a way of handling my anger and fears followed me until I was a freshman in college. I wondered if going to college, which was the first time I was able to really get away from my home, was the reason why. I now know the answer to that.

One day when I was talking to my mother, probably twenty years after I stopped passing out, I brought up how often it had happened. I thought I had a medical condition, a problem with my heart that my parents didn't care about and never discussed with me. I said I didn't have any memories of her taking me to doctors, or anyone talking to me about why this was happening or what was wrong. She stated that she had taken me to doctors and they determined there was nothing wrong with me. She went on to explain, very matter-of-factly, that I would pass out whenever I became emotionally overwrought. Looking back, this makes perfect sense: It was the only way I could deal with the unpredictability of the abuse. It was my internal structure's way of saying, "I've had enough and I'm out of here." Still, my mother's revelation stunned me.

As I left home for college, my life was hanging by a thread. I was not doing a good job at integrating into the outside world due to my internal structure being so beaten down. There was no tolerance when I begged the players in my abuse cycle to stop, and my tools were severely limited and compromised. I was experiencing numerous learning difficulties. I would go to class, but due to my internalized abusive voice being so loud, wouldn't hear what the professor was saying. It had been the same in high school, but really escalated in college. It was impossible to learn—which only deepened my sense of worthlessness and worsened my **addictions**.

I spent a lot of my young adulthood wandering aimlessly, not knowing to whom or where to turn. After all, how do you explain the madness of abuse to someone who has not experienced this reality? How could anyone understand or help if I didn't understand it myself? I never felt safe or like I had power over what was happening to me. Very much alone in my abuse, I was embarrassed by what I perceived as a weakness in my character.

As an adult, I slowly began understand my childhood anger and was finally able to not only see the little girl who stood with her fists clenched so tight, but also understand how her fists helped us survive. Many of you may hate your inner child for what happened. I do not. I'm in awe of her, standing with her fists in her never-ending quest to be heard and to fight off what she always knew was wrong. She protected me the only way she knew how, and has memories I do not. She holds all of the expanding secrets, and is great at coming up with excuses as to why we can't let go of the pain. She is tenacious and determined, though exhausted. She has earned her PhD in survival.

After looking to my wishful daydreams for inspiration and guidance, learning to love my child was one of the next steps I took in my personal healing. She never felt that anyone took care of or believed in her. All she wanted was to feel protected and loved. As an adult, it was time to help her out of her turmoil and quiet her noise. It takes vigilant, conscious thought. My adult and child were not colliding after all—they were merging. My adult consciousness fused with my child's vigilance. I had to take her reality along with my own need for growth so we could come together as one. I do not want to get rid of my child. We, as one, are a hell of a team.

On the Saturday of Memorial Day weekend, nearly two years after losing my mother, I was finally back in my mountain home after spending a month in the town where I grew up. I had been taking part in a deposition for a civil lawsuit against my stepfather for the wrongful death of my mother (which sucked), but had also gone back to gather a handful of my mother's belongings from a storage locker, something I had been forbidden to do until then. I wanted so little, yet had to fight so hard to get it. I spent the month lifting heavy boxes, moving *stuff* from house to house and figuring out how to get it home. I was cleaning my living room in preparation to lay down a rug that had been hers, something that took me almost two years to get.

Having spent weeks of heavy lifting and driving cross-country twice, I was surprised at how well I was doing. You see, since my mother's death, I have had numerous episodes of what I call total-body shut downs. I attribute them to stress, dealing with the loss of my mother and the fallout since her death. They are perhaps my adult version of passing out. I was emotionally raw when I returned home from this last trip, though I hadn't had an episode of my body shutting down in about ten months. And here on this Saturday cleaning, I moved slightly to my left and—BOOM!—I was lying on the floor, my back out, wondering if I could move.

I can't believe it, here I am again. After all the hard work I've done, with all the growth and healing I've experienced, and yet I'm back in the hole, feeling like shit. Does this ever end?

The pain this time was different. It had a crushing effect, and in more areas than before. On the floor, I became overwhelmed by my loneliness on this holiday weekend. I also knew I would have to wait until Tuesday to contact my chiropractor. Here I was, trying to put one foot in front of the other to survive the weekend, and now this. I wanted to cry, just lie there and sob, but I could not access the depth of my sadness. This work is so hard, the damage so deep and the journey long. And in that moment, I went tumbling to the bottom of the hole, head first.

Whiny, you think? Why can't I just get over this and move on? I hate the whiny. I hate the amount of work this is and how hard it has been. I hate that I still live in moments of abusive reaction when my child ignites. I hate how crushed she is, the darkness surrounding her. I hate all her ghosts. I hate that she holds on so hard and won't let go. But I understand, because she is me.

Along with the verbal and emotional abuse, I was neglected, abandoned, and not taught how to survive in the world. Unmet developmental needs hindered me from being able to form a sense of self, an identity I could call my own. I never felt I was in control of my own direction, decisions, or destiny. The leaders in my abuse cycle had a suffocating grip on me and were not about to let go, even though they were unable to exhibit true, healthy attachment. And while I always internally felt that what was happening was wrong, cruelty and invisibility was my way of life. I didn't know any other way, or what to do about it.

Even though all I wanted was to grow up and get away, I was fearful of taking chances because I had no life tools from which to draw. I needed to take cognitive steps in helping to understand what was happening to me, how to process that information, and how to solve problems by making healthier life choices. I also had to take a look at my behavior and how I was going to respond to my family cycle. I had to go back to my childhood, accept and heal the damage, and begin again. My first goal was to find my individual identity away from my family and the abuse, something I was unable to do as a child. Since I didn't have parents who did that for me, I needed to do it for myself, my child. **Autonomy**, here I come.

Memorial Day weekend made me question if things would ever change or truly get better. Would I ever reach the peaceful contentment I strive so hard to find? I had been working diligently to let go of what was and move forward. Returning to the town where I grew up had reignited all the memories of my abusive past, including having my father refuse my phone calls. At times I still treat myself as the worthless person I was made to believe I was and can't understand why I continue to do so. I know my worth, but my inner child still struggles with this at times. I am still learning how to reach my little girl, nurture her when she needs support, and bring her along on our healing path. She has so many secrets and reactions to the triggering of those raw emotions, the only ones she knows.

No matter how much I have grown as an adult, my child still reels with pain. And here she was awake once again, standing with her messy hair and tight little fists. And what set her off? I suspect she was up for a while, helping me to survive my trip in her methodical childlike way. So for that day, that weekend, I went back in and nurtured. I dealt with my frightened, irritated child who had probably spent the previous month standing with her fists, surviving each step we took. She continued to swallow her tears because it was still not safe for her to show them. I was not discounting any of the work I had accomplished up to that point. I had to deal with the exhaustion I was feeling with the constant task of letting go.

Who is my child? What is she so afraid of? Why can't she let me help her? She suffered, so I suffered. She reacted in the only way she knew how so she wouldn't disintegrate, and I fell apart. As I was climbing out of the hole this time, I again knew I had to go back inward and hug my child. I was not in the same place I was before I started my journey, but was still helping her deal with her ghosts and fears, this time as literally and figuratively paralyzing as when I had my bike accident. There's God again, still pretty smart.

I have my body blow outs and I suffer. I still struggle with her pain and with how to let us completely merge together and cry it out. Is there enough core sense, core emotionality inside of me to do this work? Why can't I just give my physical and emotional needs the gift of crying? How do I keep the belief in my capacity to do this? My inner child is primitive in her reactions and ways of dealing with that which she has always been defending. How did my family get away with this, and will I, will we, ever be able to let go?

What I learned when my back went out was that I was having a bad day and a lonely holiday weekend. My body shutting down had caused a downward spiral, sending me back

136

to the bottom of the hole. It did not undo all the good work I had done; it just stunted it for the moment. The reality and the work of growth and recovering from abuse is that my emotionality takes another hit each time my child awakens. As much as I'd like to bury my head in denial, I cannot. I must keep moving forward. And each time I comfort her, I leave the encounter with better boundaries, understanding and coping skills. And yet, each episode still pisses me off. Maybe one day my humor will prevail in these situations.

My intellectual understanding of *what is* challenges my emotional reactions, which are still so tightly bound to the painful baggage. I must continue to go back in as many times as my child needs me to and wrap my arms around her. I will continue to assure her we are a team. At times it is hard to reach her because her defenses are so wily, but I love her stubbornness. I am certain that I have to use compassion, patience, and kindness with her. How else would the adult coax the small, fragile child to move on? How does the adult help the child while she is still learning what is normal and what is not? How does the adult let her intellect help her heart?

I am better, much better, yet still working hard to keep the journey moving forward. I am determined to work with my child until we get it right. Her existence will no longer be wandering around aimlessly, reacting to her unsafe world. As I continue to find my authentic self and calm my spirit, I have had to contend with a very stubborn and frightened little girl. I love her, but when these moments occur, she is exhausting. *Kids!*

I am better, much better, yet still working hard to keep the journey moving forward. I am determined to work with my child until we get it right.

CHAPTER SIX

LETTING OURSELVES OFF THE HOOK

In the past, my internal voice was debilitating. It was loud and critical, and at times still can be.

Letting Ourselves off the Hook

Courage doesn't always roar. Sometimes courage is the quiet voice at the end of the day saying, "I will try again tomorrow."
~ Mary Anne Redmacher ~

You know that internal voice we all have, the one that guides us through life, the one we have conversations with in our head? I'm not talking about intuition this time. I'm talking about the voice our thoughts hang out in, our internal tape, the noise. In the past, my internal voice was debilitating. It was loud and critical, and at times still can be. Too many moments of my life were given away to its power. It was filled with dread, fear, and anxiety. It could be suspicious, obsessive, and paranoid, making me believe crazy things with its control. It made it hard for me to fall asleep, then woke me up at night. It was relentless, always searching for and examining the negative, the painful, the dramatic. It sounded a lot like my mother. It was my mother.

During my recovery from my bicycle accident, I knew things had to change. This was the point in my life where I started to *define* what I needed to do for myself as opposed to *asking* what I needed. No one had, after all, ever posed those types of questions to me, and I'd not done so well at listening to my own intuitive answers.

141

I had to figure out how to change my reactions during attacks and in their aftermath, especially encounters with my repeat abusers, completely aware of what I was doing and how I was doing it. I knew if I continued to live in abuse, I would have given my life to it. In other words, I would not be living at all, but withered away and internally dead. Reacting to and letting the abuse control my life was not going to be my story anymore.

I began sitting quietly to really feel the effects the encounter had on me, no matter how scary that was. I confronted my internal voice and talked to its noise, to *my* noise. I found my own loud, critical thoughts would continue the abuse by agreeing with it. I was doing to myself exactly what my abusers were doing. In those quiet moments, I realized that I had very poor self-caretaking skills and was very much reacting to abuse. I was not taking control of its impact on me. I wondered why I was giving my abusers the power and control over how I felt about myself. This is when I termed my critical voice **stinky thinking**, and I knew it had to go.

Here is how my stinky thinking worked: When attacked, my internal structure would immediately shut down. My heart would pound loudly. I'd become uncomfortable and angry as my mental torment escalated higher and higher, always ascending out of control. My self-torture would scream through the rest of that day and into the night. Sometimes it would last for days. It was never pretty. I would be livid to have let the noise affect me in such a destructive way. It exhausted me, so what was I doing out on my balcony at four in the morning? Why did this always happen? How could I stop this insanity? The older I got, the more beaten down, the stronger my internal voice became. I always left my balcony disgusted with the intrusive noise and with myself for listening to it.

Each time, I would plan how to handle the next attack. These fantasies were always so brilliant in my mind; I'd play an abusive scene over in my head and every time would have the ability to get my abuser to stop, admit their abusive ways, and apologize. I would win each encounter, and my ability to fix was perfect. In real life, however, I was never able to win, even if I thought I had found all the right words. It never occurred to me to stop trying. Or if it did, I didn't know how. My internal dialogue was stuck in the abusive attacks happening and my inability to stop them. After an attack, I always told myself that no one was going to get away with yelling at me and putting me down. Then the next attack would come and they got away with it. My situation began clouding my life in the outside world. Everyone was attacking me, no matter where they came from. My stinky thinking had become bigger than me and I felt everyone in my world was abusing me.

In the beginning, overwhelming uncertainty would cause internal and external explosions and I would have meltdowns due to my inability to gain mastery over my situation. And since this anger—mostly a cover for much deeper feelings—had as a child caused me to pass out, I worried it would again happen in my adult life. When I finally came to consciously understand my internalized abuse, I was slowly able to learn how to self-soothe as I continued to sit quietly with the effects an episode had on me. I began to calm the angry voice and started replacing it with a different one: a kinder, gentler voice that spoke of lifting me up, comforting me. It promised to not tear me down, and I did my best to trust it.

I began to understand how lucky I am to have a strong and determined constitution. This was probably the first kind thing I had ever said to myself. As I began to examine the noise of my family, I better understood the noise in my head, understood how it could be that, at times, words from my own mouth could terrify me with their cruelty. I was horrified by my total disregard for others' feelings when in my **blind rage**, rage I had learned from the abuse. The noise, both my own harsh words and those directed at me, needed to stop. My friends have described me as being blunt. It is what I have learned: saying it how I see it, direct and sometimes cruel. At times I am proud of my ability to be direct, to cut through the shit and get right to the point. It can be an effective form of communication, but in my past it was not. I am still working on my intolerant tone.

The more I was abused, the angrier I would get. Makes sense, right? Since I was unable to put my anger where it belonged, on my abusers, I learned that I would take it out on the people in my world: boyfriends, friends, and co-workers, projecting onto others what I couldn't yet put on my abusers. My anger was followed by frustration because I always struggled with the words to express what I was feeling. Hence my fades-to-black. I began to understand that I was tired of seeing my world in this way. Paralyzed by the power of abuse, I would have bouts of rage and explode on anyone in my path. I believe feeling so helpless is what would ignite me. Besides, I had learned how to be angry from my family. Intellectual understanding for me has been easy, but my emotional ability to verbally pinpoint what I was feeling was impossible. I believe this happened because when I would express my disbelief to my family over what was happening, I would be cut off, put down, and ignored. Instead of expressing my feelings verbally, I became very emotional. I never learned how to describe what I was feeling and was certain no one would listen, understand, or validate. This created the feeling that I was screaming from a mountaintop and no one could hear me. I could rant and rant and still not get to the point. At other times I would be rendered mute by my attacks and walk around numb. I'm sure people in my world just viewed me as that angry or depressed person.

My rage frightened me because I never really understood the "who" or the "why" of it. Even scarier: I didn't know what to do with it, as I'd never been given genuine permission to feel, to find and use my words to share my emotions. Scariest of all: I definitely did not know how to get rid of it.

From the time I was young and well into my late twenties, my angry outbursts caused me to go out of control. I wanted to bring down everyone around me. I never knew what would trigger an explosion. Sometimes afterward I would not know where I was, what had happened, or why. I would dissociate. This is why I understand blind rage and the danger others are in at these times. I also better understand why I passed out. I am so grateful I never physically hurt anyone, but I do understand my rages were definitely abusive to the receiver. This makes me so sad that I had the capacity to do this to others, and I am sorry to all those I hurt. What an out-of-control way to live. How *shameful* It became a part of my history that I needed to accept and forgive.

Bad habits are hard to undo. It is those steps back and learning from the fall. Since my mother's death, I've had one explosion and it cost me a wonderful friendship, a woman who is kind, gentle, and caring. To give you an idea of what a wonderful friend she was: she gave me a fiftieth birthday party, the night my mother died she was right by my side, and she took my dog in when I left for the funeral—even driving three-plus hours to an airport to fly him to me only to be told it was too hot a day and Bo could not get on the plane. She cooked for me, invited me to holiday dinners, and made me a part of her family. That is only some of the love she showed me. One day, after I returned from the funeral, she had me over, drew me a bath, and then lovingly put me in her massage chair. I fell into a peaceful sleep, overwhelmed by her kindness.

Stuffing everything I had been feeling since my mother's death, unable to say what I needed to those who caused my pain, caused me to lash out *unconsciously*, and my dear friend was on the receiving end of my rage. A couple weeks after her kindness, I went ballistic, irrationally taking all my anger and frustration with my situation out on her. It came out of nowhere and everywhere; it came from having held all that I was feeling inside. She did not deserve that, my misplaced fury, and yet she got it head on. Our friendship was irreversibly damaged that day. I miss her, our connection. We are working on reconnecting, but the blow-up will always be there. I have apologized, but words can't touch the pain I feel inside over this incident. It still horrifies me that the capacity to explode is still within. My sadness over this event still haunts, and I am so sorry to have hurt someone I love in that manner.

The only place I really had a voice was in my head, but that voice wasn't helping, supporting, or protecting me. It was continuing to abuse me by being unforgiving, critical, and chaotic. I began to sit quietly with it and realized the noise was not based in reality. It was not my authentic self, my spirit. However, it guided me with such a strong hand that it had become my reality. I was not crazy, just fighting with demons I had no part in making.

146

I began to realize my family was never going to understand my needs or the impact of their careless words. And I no longer maintained innocence when my own voice was interpreted as cruel. I couldn't do the abusive dance any longer. Most important, I realized I couldn't continue to repeat patterns I had nothing to do with forming. I understood and I couldn't deny my perpetuation of abusive behavior.

However, it did serve as a very eye-opening moment. I had to work very hard to get my anger in check and figure out how to make it work for me. I had to allow myself to be *consciously* furious, let it come up to the surface, to take my fists in a non-violent stance. I hated it and had to dig deep to find a peaceful place within me to calm all I felt. Letting go of my anger took years, but I was determined. I still have those days where I want to scream uncontrollably, especially when my abuse escalates, but I use my tools and understanding about my fears and anger to calm me so I don't explode.

If we lie to ourselves, we lie to all. If we let the stinky thinking control us, it will win and we will disappear. I knew I didn't want all the noise anymore. I didn't want *it* anymore. I had to tap into my anxieties and fears. That was where, I believed, my childhood monsters reared their ugly little heads. My loud critical voice and my anger were the first two things I had to bring out of my unconscious world and up into my conscious thought.

Looking at this and how it was affecting my life was a lesson in how to calm my spirit and get to the core of my

147

emotions while finding the words to describe and explain what I was living. I also began to understand that abuse always affects my body, mind, and spirit. I had intellectually understood this before, but I never allowed myself to feel it in an emotional way. I was too busy being tough and self-protecting to focus on my heart-mind connection, which can require diligent attention.

Work on finding your own internal dialogue, your noise, as you attempt to define the ways you take on your own abuse. The self-destruction is what keeps you stuck; it is the darkness of the hole. Use your tools to replace the more odoriferous thoughts with any words that more accurately represent the pure beauty of your true, genuine self. Allow your internal noise to be your own—you're the only one, after all, who can hear it. You're in total control.

When I'd become angry in the past and try to take down everyone in my path, I was unable to step outside myself and take a good look at my behavior. I had convinced myself that the cause of my anger was always justified; it was someone else's fault and they deserved my outbursts. I could always justify my behavior, just like my abusers could justify theirs. This was the way I had been taught to cope: by not taking any responsibility for my actions. However, as I began to learn about my observing ego, I understood my participation in my life and its outcomes. At first I would simply watch, as if an outside observer, my out-of-control angry outbursts. It took a while to convince myself that I was responsible for my reactions to what I was feeling and I could no longer blame the outside world or my abusers for them. I had earned my anger, so letting go was a struggle. Striking out supplemented my comfort in my discomfort.

When I began to understand the reality that my life had become merely waiting for the next blows, I understood I was living a life always being on guard.

I'd react to what I perceived as abuse and the outside world would be confused and put off by my reaction. I stood with tightening fists so long, I didn't know how to unclench them. They were my protection and survival. I was slowly able to start stepping outside of myself and began to watch how I was handling my rage. It was not pretty. I was so beaten down and had no tools with which to change my situation. I felt powerless, worthless, and enraged by this. What I saw shocked and disgusted me and it had to change, or I felt I would be lost forever. So I chose life, change, and growth.

When I would blow, I would sit with myself and focus on my triggers that led to the explosion. It made me sick that I was being abusive to people through my angry rages. I was repeating the behaviors of all my abusers, behaviors I had nothing to do with starting. It had to stop. I began to understand that most of the people in my life outside of my family were not being cruel or abusive. They were reacting to my unpredictability and rage. I was always so ready to be abused that I reacted to every situation as though it was abusive. I still consciously stay aware of the triggers that used to set me off. I still stumble and make mistakes in life situations that I think are abusive, but I am aware and no longer have rage-filled outbursts. Well, almost never.

After my bike accident, I began to protest the harshness of words my family used to attack me. Actually, I think I had been challenging my experience with abuse my whole life, but now I was conscious of what I was objecting too. My feelings always baffled them. If I disputed the abusive behavior, they simply ignored me. When I asked them to stop, I was met with total disregard. Explaining I was hurt would only escalate the attacks. When I'd tell them I didn't want to participate in the madness anymore, they couldn't hear me. They never gave thought to the delivery of what they said, no matter how vicious. Once the merciless words are put out there, the damage is done. It was getting harder to forgive my abusers and move on, and I couldn't protect myself from their verbal blows. Their inability to hear debilitated me, cut to my core, and continued to destroy my sense of self, only escalating the noise in my head. Only now, I was finally putting my foot down.

Often I'd tell the noise to shut the fuck up. I would say that to myself internally and at times out loud. If you ever saw a woman walking down the street and suddenly screaming out loud *shut the fuck up!* that was me, looking up to the sky, confronting my noise. It was my frustration and exhaustion—with living a life never feeling safe, never trusting, still holding on to the trauma—getting the best of me.

At first I was furious that when I told the noise to leave me alone, all it did was provoke it more and push me deeper into the hole. I viewed my fears and anxieties as a separate entity, something to be rid of, like throwing out the trash. But the noise was truly a part of me. I didn't understand I was only aggravating myself by attacking one of my child's survival skills. She became enraged at my intrusion into the only way she knew how to live. I was doing the same thing to her that my abusers were doing to me. She'd simply had enough and didn't want to be messed with. She was too tired to fix or change anything. She couldn't, as she was just a little girl.

As I learned how to sit in quiet solitude listening to my noise, instead of being distracted by external sounds, I began the process of understanding the stranglehold it had on my life. I had never allowed myself one moment of peace. In those meditative moments, the chaos would be gone. The quiet was amazing. The more I sat with the noise, the calmer I became. I thought about my child and what she endured, all she had fought off with her tenacity and grit. More importantly, I began to understand all she was unable to fight off or stop from happening and began to share sorrow over how scared and brave she was. Our fear was the same, as was our courage.

In those moments, I knew I had to change how I viewed my internal structure, noise and all, and love it for being my guide all those years, my survival system. Instead of being angry, I began to accept my child's inability to escape the noise in her head. I was compassionate and loving. I'd never really had that before, and it felt great. I engaged with, embraced, and honored my struggle. I was tolerant, even in those moments when the noise would escalate. I began to take in all we had spent our lifetime running from. This took time, but I stuck with it. There were many moments—and sometimes are still—when I felt the internal work was too hard and wanted to stop, but I continued to hold strong in my determination and need for change. As I got to know my little girl and understand her struggles, I began the process of being grateful to her and honoring all that distressed her. I was blown away by her strength.

And then I got it.

I started out thinking I had to get rid of *it*. Then I understood that getting rid of *it* would be getting rid of me and my existence, my child. By telling my noise to get lost and go away, I was telling *her* to get lost and go away. Thank God for all the years of her standing with fists, not allowing me to be rid of her. I fell in love, real love, unconditional and protective love. That was the first time I understood what love was. It was the first time I had love without a connection to abuse. How can anything abusive be connected to love? Once I understood that, I could finally see my child and all that came with her. It was the first time I believe she felt seen.

I had to begin asking myself how I could quiet the noise, replace it with powerful words of self-enhancement, and get to a place of internal empowerment. I had to learn that I was not what my abusers were saying, but strong, powerful, loving, kind, and compassionate. I had to let myself off the hook for listening to the stinky thoughts for so many years. I had to let myself off the hook for my blind rages while accepting responsibility for changing my own abusive habits and tendencies. I had to allow myself to believe in my ability to believe in myself. It wasn't easy and I had to be constantly aware, but eventually the noise began to quiet and the episodes did not last as long.

When my body responds to abusive encounters, which are now becoming the exception and not the rule, I continue being my own parent and nurture myself. Now most of the time when it comes up, I am able to define what ignited it, talk and walk myself through it, and come out the other end. I've made the noise okay, because why wouldn't I have it? I normalized this reaction for myself and I began taking steps to move away from it. I still experience this today, only I am able to quiet it much quicker and move away from the internal effects. I am learning how to let go of that which is out of my control. If the stinky thinking enters my mind, it doesn't last very long anymore.

On the days nothing works, usually right after a verbal and emotional bashing, I just leave it alone. I stay out **of the noise's way** and let it be. I take my child's fists and massage them out. Sometimes it works, sometimes it doesn't. When it doesn't work, I will talk to my friends and my therapist. By engaging in things other than the stinky thinking, by ignoring the nagging, it leaves much more quickly. If I am still a mess, the monsters attacking with a vengeance, I try to do nothing and just stay quiet. But when I ignore the intuitive knowledge of my need to do nothing, those days are steps backwards. I now make it okay when I take steps back. What I am learning now is how to nurture this part of me without the fear that I will be crushed if I show my authentic self. I am also learning who my authentic self is and trusting those I choose to have in my life to treat me with kindness and respect. Unlearning unhealthy behaviors is hard, but learning healthy ones is the real work. And remember: we're only human.

By engaging in things other than the stinky thinking, by ignoring the nagging, it leaves much more quickly. If I am still a mess, the monsters attacking with a vengeance, I try to do nothing and just stay quiet.

CHAPTER SEVEN

MOTHER DAUGHTER DANCE

Five years after I left my family for the mountains, the cycle of abuse continued, but the distance allowed me more space to start defining my new normal.

MOTHER-DAUGHTER DANCE

"Intuition will tell the thinking mind where to look next."
~ Jonas Salk ~

Five years after I left my family for the mountains, the cycle of abuse continued, but the distance allowed me more space to start defining my new normal. At first, after every abusive encounter I had with family members (by now mostly on the phone), I would react by entering a numb state. It felt like an out-of-body experience, as if I was able to separate myself from myself. I felt confused by the power, the quickness of the assaults and by their ability to disorient and disconnect me from reality. This dissociative reaction would happen whether I was prepared for the attack or not. However, the difference was that this time I was paying attention and learning. When the abuse would happen, I went straight to the safe, beautiful mountains where I was able to sit peacefully, breathe, and hike. I was learning how to quiet and calm the stinky thinking, learning how to control my anger. I was reconnecting with myself to stay on my journey towards health.

When my mother would visit me, which she did often, my ability to tolerate and not personalize the assaults strengthened. I learned how to separate out what was hers and what was mine.

The verbal barrages continued, but their effects lessened. They always hurt and made me sad, yet were no longer crippling. I was growing up and no longer accepting what was not mine. I was beginning to learn how to have her in my life and not let her destroy my spirit, something I was still working on the day she was killed.

However, as I began letting go, I didn't know how to protect myself. Again, I wondered if you could buy this tool at a store. I realized I had spent a lifetime of screaming openly and dramatically, both within my family and out in the world. I was still, in many ways, the same fearful child, riddled with invisible broken bones and scar tissue. For too many years, every step I made or breath I took, I carried those scars within my fractured being, blaming myself for the abuse. I would try to fix it, and it still would not stop.

I never want to become complacent to the attacks of abuse. I needed to get to a point where I refused to do the same thing with the same result. Insanity, it has been said, is repeating behavior while expecting a different outcome. I understood getting out of the hole would not happen overnight. My mother loved me and my family loves me the only way they know how. This is not said as an excuse for them, but the reality of the situation. Leaving the cycle required strength and determination and I now have my tools. I fell a lot at first and I still fall at times, but I can now climb out of the hole. I've found another street, with smaller holes, and that's life.

The year before she was killed, I went to my mother's for Thanksgiving. I had to, the intuitive pull too strong to ignore. When I arrived, her anxiety was off the chart. She was angry, hostile, overwhelmed, and scared. She seemed to be slowly disintegrating, and I had to try to do something about it. This was my lifetime pattern of trying to fix and never succeeding. The wrath of her anger was directed towards me, always me. I couldn't get her to slow down long enough to look and see how out of control her situation had become. I knew my time with her was limited. I had known for a while. How? I just did.

My mother did not want me to come back for the holiday, and was very angry that I had done so. I believe she didn't want me to see the chaos in her life. I had recently begun to ask her to slow down and take a look at Jack's deteriorating health, his escalating rage and the impact it was having on her. I believed he was having mini-strokes called transient ischemic attacks (TIA) and was in the early stages of dementia. Every time I brought my concerns, she became enraged. She would not discuss it with me, simply stating that each time Jack was hospitalized, it was pneumonia. I did not believe her explanations, but she held firm to her stance on his health issues. He was beginning to scare me, yet she was resistant to my pleas to deal with his health.

Jack was just getting out of the hospital, and a health care worker was moving in to help. In spite of that, my mother was still planning a large Thanksgiving dinner with family and friends and I wanted to take part since I was alone far away. While there, I continued to beg her to leave her relationship. I begged and begged for her to calm down enough so we could talk. She exploded before my eyes in a mass of hysteria. I attempted to calm her rage until I too finally broke.

159

She yelled at me about everything, whether it had to do with me or not. She belittled me, cut me down, and told me I was worthless and unwelcome at her home for Thanksgiving. It was her words of hatred and disgust flung at me with unknowing, or uncaring, disregard for their impact. As an isolated incident, it may not have mattered, but this was fifty years of verbal and emotional abuse, compounded. She complained about a cousin who had also come to stay at the house who had not been welcome either. However, she shared all her rage with me, never my cousin.

One morning, the same cousin and I were cleaning up the kitchen after breakfast, only to have my mother barrel in, grab dishes out of my hand, rewash them, and reload the dishwasher. This was something she had done since I was a little girl, complaining about how I did the dishes wrong. I wiped my hands on a cheap Costco dishtowel hanging on the door, which sent my mother into another rage about how the dishtowel was there for decoration. How dare I dry my hands on a dishtowel hanging on the door? My cousin watched this interaction and thought it was funny and made jokes about it. Even though I laughed and went along with it, I was dying inside.

Later, again in the kitchen, my mother went into yet another rage. The words of hatred shot into my heart with bow-and-arrow precision. Crushed, I stood immobile by the dining room table as she verbally attacked me with a vengeance, unable to see the effects to my spirit. I was unable to use my defenses after this attack, my emotions caught in my throat and blocking my air supply. I went in to the bedroom, my mother following closely after me. I wanted to pack my bags and go home, but I couldn't get away from her. She went into yet another rage about the bedroom my cousin and I were sharing. She wanted it spotless, she said, although—especially as an adult—I had always been respectful of my mother's need for a clean home. Though my side of the room was tidy, my cousin's was not. Regardless, I was blamed for the mess while my cousin went on a meditative walk, oblivious to my mother's emotionality. Unable to acknowledge—or perhaps even see—my turmoil, my mother continued her cruel attack. I couldn't understand why this woman hated me so much. I couldn't understand how she was unable to see what she was doing to me, had always done to me. As I once again absorbed her abuse, my emotions were on their knees in devastation. At this, the tears I had stuffed for a lifetime came flooding out.

I fell into a puddle, the kind of cry where the sobs take your breath away and strange noises emerge from deep within. It had been about twenty-seven years since I had cried out loud in that way. Real tears gushed down my cheeks. I was broken by my stands-with-fists position, for up until that moment, I had mostly cried **invisible tears**. The water I had kept hidden behind the dam finally came flooding out. My emotions during that visit were so thick with fear, I could no longer remain silent. This felt like the worst episode I'd ever experienced at my mother's hand, and I broke. As I cried, my mother became angry. She told me, screamed at me, to stop. She couldn't handle it, afraid of my tears and sadness. This time I couldn't stop, wouldn't stop. I could no longer swallow my pain nor suspend my needs in order to make her feel better. I was livid with how disrespectful and cruel she was, and angry with her request for me to stop crying, which had finally made me *visible* to her. I could no longer deal with her anxiety, anger, and attacks. I was done. Where was the mother to hug me in my tears and sadness? Where was the mother I needed to listen to me? I told her I would not stop crying and emphatically stated there was nothing wrong with my tears. I told her I was sad, beyond concerned about her, and depleted of energy. When she stopped long enough to see my sobs, she did hug me. She calmed for a moment. That was a first. My tears subsided briefly as I attempted to take in her hug, the hug from the mother of my dreams. A split second later, she was off again in her rage.

Thanksgiving was a bust, except for that brief hug. Fleeting as it was, it was a hug for the little girl still longing for her mommy's love at fifty years old. It was incredibly sad for my young child and pathetic to me as an adult. As I stood there in disbelief at that brief moment of tenderness, and at how I couldn't believe I had spent all those years with her being uncomfortable with my tears, all those years of invisibly crying. In that moment, I refused to stop feeling. I would no longer allow her to force me to swallow my sadness. I went home extremely afraid for my mother, but done being a target of her rage.

My mother made me feel like an intruder, an unwanted guest during my visit. I know it seems like she was reacting to typical stress and was anxious due to her current circumstances, which she was, and with good reason. The difference is this was her consistent behavior with me over the course of my life: raging at me, never really seeing, listening, or allowing me to have a voice. Still, she would always turn to me as her emotional guide when moments of uncertainty and sadness would hit. The one thing she really did respect about me was my abilities as a therapist. This paradox was most confusing, always. On the one hand, she held me up on a pedestal for my professional talents, and then personally beat me down, never wanting to take a look at *our* issues.

She constantly yelled at me about everything, except when others were around. Jack heard it because he was there and participated in his own forms of abuse with my mother, yet the abuse was always done behind closed doors. If others saw, they chose to not interfere. When I would ask her how she could speak to me with such disregard to my feelings and spirit, she would deflect the question and go off about some other way I failed, continuing to stomp on my spirit. I always internalized this: I was worthless, stupid, and unworthy of having thoughts and feelings of my own. Dissociation often prevents me from remembering the exact words, but it never can protect from the memory of how I felt. Upon reflection of her attack at Thanksgiving, I realize it was probably the first encounter where I was consciously taking in the attack instead of dissociating and going numb, consciously aware of the abusive behavior and unwilling to make any more excuses to myself for it.

I left thinking I had to figure out a way to break things off with my mother if she would not change. I was done being a target of her rage and carrying all of it alone. My ability to tolerate the acceptance of the unacceptable came crashing down. Once home, I thought a lot about the fact that I had finally cried tears I had been denying myself for so many years. It cost me when I moved away from the center of my emotionality and my tough exterior became my greatest asset. My belief that displaying vulnerability and sadness was a weakness was seriously flawed, and my heart and spirit paid the price. What had happened to break that dam wide open? I had to go back more than twenty years to see why the tears had stopped.

I stopped crying in my early twenties after a very disturbing event. Crying did me no good because my family, especially my mother, was either discomforted or didn't care about my pain and tears. I had to become so tough, I actually believed in my toughness. Any weakness was futile for me to express, as these feelings were consistently met with total disregard, if not harsh criticism. Anger and rage were fine—the louder the better. Vulnerability was not.

On this day, a man I was dating became verbally, emotionally, and almost physically violent with me—my cycle of abuse repeating. I ran to my mother for her love, support, and help. I was crying hard and shaking with fear. Instead of showing the compassion I so desperately needed, my mother became overwhelmed and anxious. She could not handle my pain.

I had caught her on her way out of her house when she was going to yet another "very important meeting." This time she became angry with me for making her late. I felt so alone in my disbelief. She refused to miss her volunteer board meeting to stay with me. I ended up going with her because, so afraid and shaken, I felt I couldn't be alone. As I sat through this meeting, embarrassed and invisible, I wondered how it could be more important than me. It was on that day, I remembered, that I had made a rash decision, one I came to regret: I decided to stop crying.

My maternal grandmother died more than a decade later, I was thirty-eight, and I was a mess. My love for her was huge. The one person in the world who I felt truly loved me, who saw and cared about me, was gone. I was consumed by my grief, yet my family was unable to sit with sadness and just mourn. In the days preceding and the day of the funeral, I was treated with emotional cruelty from several members within my family system. Here we

164

were adults, and I felt no one noticed or questioned the behavior, not even the rabbi.

We decided to only have a gravesite funeral. Days before, I tried to play the song "Somewhere," by Barbra Streisand, for my mother. I planned to play it at the funeral. It was yet another attempt to connect with her in a meaningful way. The song started, she listened for a split second, turned the CD player down and proceeded to make a phone call. *So much for "the moment."*

At the funeral, I hit the play button and went to one of the chairs set up for family members. I just wanted to sit, listen to the beautiful words with that soothing music as they put my grandmother's ashes in the ground. I just wanted to feel. As my mother came to sit next to me, she began quietly yelling about how I had to make things better with the person who had been being so emotionally abusive to me. Up until that moment, no one had seemed to notice this cruelty or said anything about it. I couldn't believe what was happening. They were burying my grandmother—her mother—and I wasn't given permission to feel, cry, or mourn. I was being yelled at for being abused. I again shut my tears down. The funeral was over for me.

It's hard to cry when you have only learned how to keep your sadness at bay, blocked with a brick wall so no one may see your vulnerability. I missed out on a lot by disallowing my tears. I viewed it as bravery; I thought I was courageous. I was wrong; I was only surviving. I had learned how to be a coward, for it takes actual strength to show sadness through tears. It takes real courage to show vulnerability during weak moments of the spirit.

I've spent so much of my life alone in my pain. If we are ignored, if others become uncomfortable in the presence of our pain, or if the abuse escalates because we show it, we begin to question if it is okay to feel such things. When our feelings are shut down at an early age, we especially don't know how to deal. What I learned was how to stay stuck, swallow my feelings and walk away from encounters feeling worthless because I believed no one cared how I felt. I was always looking for comfort in those hurtful and confusing moments, but there was none to be had. I began to fear the longing for kindness, that loving touch or those encouraging words. Stuck in my family cycle, I lost sight of those outside the circle who are not afraid of my tears. I missed out because of my own fear of opening up.

I still fear abandonment and that no one will care. I would give anything to have somebody hold me in my pain. Rock me until I calm. Allow me to let go of the sadness that has been my life and tell me I will be okay. Release me from a lifetime filled with sorrow, hurt, regret, and the belief I was unlovable. I am getting to a place where I can let go of what I could not control and forgive myself. My goal is to let go of all I was unable to change. I am giving myself permission to allow vulnerability and tears back into my life. I now know I must find that within myself first and foremost. I am getting better and still learning how to do this. I will get there. And yet, I still have not really cried for my mother since she died. I do have teary moments, but other than Thanksgiving I have not been able to let go of my stuffed tears. What I now know is that by taking crying out of my emotionality, I was left with the inability to self-soothe and have since had difficulty showing my emotions, or even knowing what I am feeling.

I've been learning—am still learning—how to work through rough patches. For you, it may be something completely different. As an adult, I cannot blame anyone but myself now for my shutting down. In my journey to find wholeness, I search for my tears.

A few months after the Thanksgiving trip, I was called to where my mother spent time in the winter. I was pulled to her again, the feeling that she needed me so strong. I went for a week and stayed almost a month. Though I thought I'd decided I was done after the Thanksgiving fiasco, apparently my concern, worry, and love for my mother overpowered my need to take care of myself. I was still trying to fix.

What I walked into was potent distress filled with fear and rage so thick I could hardly breathe. Jack was being abusive, so cruel with his words and tone. His anger was directed towards my mother and at times towards me. His large stature was becoming so out of control that I felt his rages were becoming physical. Though his health—both mentally and physiologically—was deteriorating, his physical strength and height were much bigger than my tiny mother. It was scary to watch. Others in her social circle were also beginning to wonder if Jack was becoming physically abusive.

I was shocked and saddened by my mother's appearance. Yes, she was seventy-seven, but she suddenly looked old to me. Her vibrant energy with which she plowed through life was dimming. That did not stop her or slow her down, but she was depleted nonetheless. In the two months since I had seen her, she had been so beaten down, her shoulders hunched and her eyes reflecting pain and defeat. Things were bad—very bad—during Thanksgiving. Now they were worse.

It was an odd month filled with incredible extremes. A short time into my stay, I began again begging her to leave Jack, the request I had made often in the past couple of years. I couldn't understand why she wanted to stay with a man who had the capacity for such verbal and emotional cruelty. Her pride was so large, her ability to be beaten down just as big. I was tired of watching it. I was tired of her embodying this type of role model. I also begged her to tell Jack's children. I begged her to tell her friends. She just became defensive and abusive at my pleas. Maybe that's where I learned how to stand with fists, as my feet were encased in concrete over the danger of which I was now a part. In those moments, her equally cemented stance of denial at her situation was fierce: our crazy mother-daughter dance.

Every attempt I made to pack and go home was futile. I could no more leave my mother than she could let me go. The first week became the second week, became the third and fourth. She maintained her maddening energy through all of this, still planning events and parties, going to educational classes and bringing her neighborhood together, the gift of her lifetime of running. But this time it came from a different place. It broke my heart to see how beaten down and tired she was and know I couldn't do anything to change her situation. At the other end of this was Jack: angry, sullen, and unkind.

He would rage, she would rage. He would scream and she would scream. They were out of control. A male caretaker came with them to take care of Jack and drive for him was also on the receiving end of their verbal and emotional attacks, as was I. They made my dog cry and shake with fear. I couldn't help, yet I couldn't leave. The caretaker and was grateful that I kept extending my stay. I asked him why he didn't just quit. He needed the money and felt he had to endure what was happening.

My mother's anger was escalating to new levels, even for me. This time it was choking her little body, tearing her apart internally and externally. It was disastrous trying to slow my mother down and get her to face the seriousness of her situation. She would not allow my words to resonate. I kept having the unshakable fear that he was going to hurt or kill her in an accident, and had told her so too many times to count. I knew I would not have her—and she knew she would not be here—for long. I honestly believe that on some level she knew she was going to die if she stayed, yet remained unable to leave. I wanted to run away, leave the madness and bury my head in the sands of denial. I truly believe I was the only one in our family seeing the madness of her life, mostly invisible to others. Or maybe the others in my family were so used to the destruction and anger they no longer noticed. The responsibility of seeing and not being able to change the situation clenched me with a mind-numbing intensity.

One event in particular made it clear I would not have her long. She was very agitated with Jack, and I watched her pace through their home, stating repeatedly how he had been lying to her about money for years. When they bought the house, she told me, Jack kept telling her he was broke. We walked from room to room as my mother ranted about paying for all the furniture in the house. If anything happened to her, I needed to get all of her possessions. She did this for days. "Make sure you get my stuff if anything happens to me." Finally, in the midst of her craziness about her stuff, I had her write down everything to get her to stop obsessing. We walked from room to room as she wrote down, item by item, what things were hers and what was his. She looked at each piece of furniture, rug, dish, pot, pan, and piece of art. We decided she would do this with me over the phone when she returned to their other home.

I was never worried about division of property with Jack's children. My relationship with them was built in trust and love. It was something I had spoken to his daughter about several times, and we made a pact to never fight about what was his or hers. I made the list because I was watching my mother go crazy before my eyes. She kept a copy and I kept a copy. I kept thinking how bizarre the scene was. If she would have just left with me, she could have taken her stuff and I'd still have her. *The stuff!* That's what her life had become. Those words—*make sure you get my stuff*—still haunt me.

I've never considered my mother the nurturing type, but we were closely tied. I knew my time with her was limited, that I would never see her again after I left. It was written on banners in large bold letters all over my universe. So, every night, I would request all the palatable meals I had in a lifetime with her (the ones that didn't require massive amounts of ketchup). I had never made requests like these before: her lamb chops, meatloaf, grilled steaks and chicken, her carrots and green beans with brown sugar and butter, her squash, and especially her tuna fish salad, my comfort food with my mother. Every night we ate at home, she made one of those meals. Every night I savored every morsel, knowing it was my last.

I also made sure we had some good and relaxing moments together—at least as relaxing as my mother could be.

We signed up for educational classes together. We went to movies and an opera. We shopped at Costco. (She *loved* Costco.) We went for walks with Bo and to the putting green to hit golf balls at the range. Several evenings, we would sign up to be the last group on the course so we could take our time and watched the sunset. Every night, either my mother would come into my bedroom, or Bo and I would go into hers to hug, kiss, and tell each other how much we loved each other and how glad we were that I was there. We'd never done that before. I have to believe we both knew our time together was ending. And each night as I lay in bed, I cried invisible tears. I was still holding on.

I continued to beg her to come with me, to pack her bags, get in my car and just leave. She would not. I begged her to let his children know how bad the situation had become, how dangerous it was. She tried: Jack's daughter and son-in-law flew in while I was there. My mother kept telling them there were problems. They came, listened, and did not see the stranglehold. Did they choose not to notice? Feel there was nothing they could do? Couldn't they smell the danger of it all? I couldn't understand their behavior. Then they left. Strike one for help.

Jack's son and daughter-in-law lived close to their winter home and came over one day for brunch. I had been there almost three weeks at this point, and this was their first visit to see their father since I'd arrived. My mother shopped, planned, brought out the good dishes, and created a beautiful setting for this meal. It had to look perfect. The presentation had to be just right. She became enraged with me when I attempted to help, of course, because I never *could* do anything right.

171

The purpose of the brunch was to discuss what was going on with his father, how out of control everything had become. They came; the conversation began. The women remained in the kitchen setting up the lunch while Jack and his son spoke in the bedroom for about a half hour. I listened outside the door, but could not tell what they were saying. As they exited the room, his son announced, "He will not tell me about his finances, so there is nothing I can do." His finances? What about his behavior? His son was done. Strike two.

No help was offered by either child. I wanted to scream with a megaphone into their faces, wanted to explode with the same craziness I'd been watching. Couldn't they feel the stress? Couldn't they see how depleted my mother had become? Did they even try? I wanted to run away. I wanted to lash out in anger. I wanted to let my mother's dirty secrets out, but I could not. It would have devastated and embarrassed her. I stood in stunned silence watching all of my mother's demons unfold: all her secrets, and I, the unwitting accomplice.

The morning I left my mother's house, we were both very sad. I did not want to leave, but it was time. I spent the morning pleading with her to pack a bag and come with me. She could not. I again begged her to tell her neighbor, a close friend, what was going on. She could not. My final request was her tuna fish for me to take on my long drive home. She had never made me a "to go" package before. I had never asked, but that morning she did and filled it with everything she knew I loved.

As I packed my car, my ability to breathe diminished. I wanted to run to her neighbor's house and let them know my mother was in danger, but I was paralyzed into submission. She had warned me not to tell because of the embarrassment others finding out about her situation would cause. She was always begging me—or raging at me—not to tell. All those secrets, the power of abuse, what a deadly burden. We hugged tight and for longer than we ever had before. I was defeated, and she had "won."

Abuse won.

She stood in the driveway as I pulled out. I looked at her, taking all of her in. As I started down the street, I stopped to look back at her through my rearview mirror, knowing it was the last time I would see her.

She waved, as if in slow motion.

Stuck in a bad B-movie, I cried my invisible tears all the way home.

That was the last time I saw my mother. Four months later, she was dead.

What I learned from the events leading up to my mother's death was to listen to my intuition. I wonder if I had, if I'd told the secrets and screamed out my concerns, if anything would have been different. I don't know; I'll never know. I have no choice but to let that go. I also understand that I spent a lifetime putting aside my own needs and emotions along with my professional and intellectual understanding to try to fix my family cycle of abuse.

What a waste of time! I should have been working on myself and doing the things that I needed for my own sanity and growth. I've squandered so much of my life trying to fix and feeling stuck, failing at the impossible. In moments of anger I want to scream, "Fuck 'em all!"

During the craziness of the last two years of my mother's life, I learned that I was unable to truly take care of myself. I allowed my family to tear me down by taking their cruelty to heart. With this understanding, I decided I would no longer participate in the abuse cycle. My mother was dead and I no longer had to participate in this self-destructive behavior. The challenge of changing the game has been grueling at times. Yet I am slowly coming into my own with my rules, my voice, and my choices.

In the last four months of her life, I stopped trying to have a voice in my family, stopped trying to be heard. There was no point in continuing the aggravation. In my family, anger was always acceptable—the louder, the better. It is what I learned. Sadness, pain, and vulnerability were either not attended to or viewed as weakness. I now understand what an enormous undertaking it is to access those feelings and let them surface. I was well on my way by now to discovering my authentic self. I knew I needed to see the whole enchilada—with all my beauty marks and warts—and remain committed in my journey towards growth. I had so far been able to take a close look at the reality I was living and begin to coax my child onto my side while challenging my critical internal voice. I decided to look at each part of the good, the bad, and the ugly separately so my intellect wouldn't overtake my emotionality. I had to find a way to bring them together. I needed to figure out the normal rhythm of life and calm all my inherent intense emotional reactions to its highs and lows; I needed to find my balance in the dance.

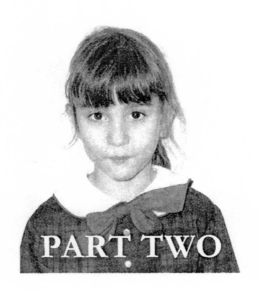

PART TWO

Part I has focused mostly on my relationship with my mother as I perceived it. After she died, however, my abusive situation escalated to epic proportions that were very frightening to me.

Again, I do not wish to call people out on the carpet or play the blame game. *I have no interest in something so counterproductive.* This is simply the story of how *I* came to terms with the abuse in *my* life, took responsibility for my part in it, and grew up. "The role of a writer," to quote Anaïs Nin, "is not to say what we can all say, but what we are unable to say."

CHAPTER EIGHT

VOMITOTUS-TOO-MUCHUS

When confronted with chaos, I try to take it in, to feel it all, but it is so overwhelming that I have to compartmentalize in order to figure out what I am experiencing.

VOMITOTUS-TOO-MUCHUS

*"Never be bullied into silence. Never allow yourself to be made a victim.
Accept no one's definition of your life; define yourself."*
~ Harvey Fierstein ~

When confronted with chaos, I try to take it in, to feel it all, but it is so overwhelming and devastating that I have to compartmentalize in order to figure out exactly what I am experiencing. In my attempts to feel—or to avoid feeling pain—I fracture off into many pieces so as not to be engulfed, my moments of dissociation. It makes it difficult for me to truly know what I am feeling in the moment. At times, my thoughts can be so guarded; the ability to see things clearly and really absorb them became all but impossible. Eventually, the emotions bubble up in spurts—or crash in like tidal waves—making it difficult to truly access or define, still, what I feel. In the past, when I *did* see clearly and was able to articulate my thoughts, my abusers made sure I knew I was wrong: I was crazy.

I've mentioned the importance of humor in my life, and indeed much of it has been sarcastic in nature. I try not to downplay the very real pain we feel when we are abused, or are recovering, but sometimes it comes out sounding that way. I would hate to sound flippant. Being pelted with verbal assaults *and* internalized abuse all at once is a lot to process, so the result can be a cascade of thoughts, feelings, and words all spilling out at once. This I call ***vomitotus-too-muchus.***

179

In the hours after my mother died, I was pulled back down into the hole. It happened very quickly, and while I understood intellectually, my heart went into overdrive and I had trouble catching up. When, at the bistro, I received the call delivering the news, Barney drove me back to my brother's house. Nothing made sense. I couldn't feel. Two different people seemed to be colliding into the present moment: the person I was before her death and the one I wanted to become. This experience facilitated a whole new level of my own personal growth and learning. It caused me to look back on my life: my defenses, my fears, and my courage.

This is probably the hardest thing I will ever admit. It is the most vulnerable and powerful thing I will ever do for myself in acknowledging this. Many from the world of my mother may not understand what I am saying, but I do. I cannot ask you, the reader, to dig deep, be honest with yourself and deal with your ghosts, if I am not willing to do so as well. It is all part of my journey, the same journey I am asking you to give yourself permission to embark upon. What we feel is very raw and undeniably real. My own feelings, that night, had nothing to do with the love, loss, and complete devastation I felt learning how my mother died, coping with the fact that someone I loved so deeply was gone. It had to do with something much more powerful.

All the external forces were coming at me, and it was simply too much. My need to just be still, feel, and mourn were wiped out in an instant. I knew the situation was going into the darkness, and I needed to figure out how to self-protect. Stunned by the display of chaos, anger, and sadness surrounding me, and also in shock, I tried to access my true feelings about the experience without getting sucked back down. Actually, I couldn't feel anything while feeling everything all at once. How familiar: the oxymoronic vomitotus-too-muchus!

Yet, a calm voice in my head weeded through all the darkness in those moments. It was a gentle and kind voice, a spirit if you will. It was my child and I coming together in our time of grief, and, in that internal place, I knew relief. Everything I thought in that moment conflicted with all I felt, but I found a calm I had never sensed before.

I was finally free. My suffering was over. My abusive existence was done. Since my mother was the only reason I had put up with the abuse, her death freed me. I knew I was no longer willing to participate in anything harmful or destructive to my personal health and happiness. I knew I was done being a participant in abusive forces I had nothing to do with. The last two years of her life had been exhausting for me as I begged her to leave Jack, my intuition screaming that he was going to kill her, whether intentionally or not. Though crushed that I'd been right, and profoundly saddened that *I* could not have stopped it, in a heartbeat, I realized my existence in abuse was finally done.

As I try to come to terms with these feelings of reprieve, I've begun to understand the depth of what I am going through. When I think about my mother and her power to verbally and emotionally abuse me, I wonder if I would have ever been able to break free from her grip of power and control. Moving away helped, but I was still in her grasp. I now understand that I would have continued to be the perpetual little girl trying to get my mommy's love and approval. I would have stayed until she loved me. I would have stayed in the abuse, *unconsciously chosen* to stay. I will need to nurture this part of me forever, let myself off the hook for feeling it and know that I have every reason to. My sadness over this is immense, a void inside me I nurture every day, but the relief is real. It is. How devastating that my mother's death delivered freedom. Though this revelation is still enough to bring me to my knees, my understanding is intact.

With my revelation of freedom somewhere inside guiding me, chaos detonated all around. The fallout from my mother's death hit a level of drama that only could have been orchestrated by her. It was all-encompassing and exhausting. Everyone in the cycle had their own reactions. I knew my boundaries were clearer and my willingness to shoulder the burdens of abuse was lessening. But right after she died, everything I knew took a hit.

Back in the hole, I made sure my ladder was there for me to climb out as soon as the opportunity presented itself, for the darkness was not mine; it was just all around me. I was in shock and feeling a depth of loss I had never felt before. How to deal without getting swallowed up again? In that moment, the hole became my salvation. This time, I consciously used it *as a tool* to protect myself, like a soldier in the trenches, to all that was happening around me.

I decided it would be better for the moment to get along, agree, and fix than to stand up for my rights, to have a voice. I allowed dissociation to happen. I was attempting to balance dramatic escalation while attending to my own safety and sanity. It was grueling to want to be there for my family, though certain I would drown in their system. And from past experience, I knew I was about to take this journey alone.

I tossed and turned in bed that night, struggling not to let my fragile emotional state consume me. Fear was competing with overwhelming sadness. All I wanted was to sit quietly and cry, figure out what I was feeling, and try to mourn this impossible tragedy, but that did not happen. I had to put aside my need to mourn in order to survive. It couldn't just be about my mother and her death. It was a situation in which I wasn't really given a choice, not that I had ever been during a family crisis or period of mourning. I was desperate not to undo all the internal work I had done and was unwilling to go back into the dark sadness of a life filled with abuse—my critical tape blasting on loop. I was already being pulled downward. When I arrived for the funeral, closer to sea level, I knew the rest of the tug would be waiting. The only thing I knew for certain was another paradox: Even though I was back in the hole, I wasn't going down again. I thought it would be temporary.

I always justified this behavior—pacifying in order to survive—by convincing myself it was easier. It wasn't. It never is. It never will be. Intellectually, I knew what was going on around me, but had to remain numb. I needed my shell. The difference this time? I was *consciously* unconscious, attempting to simply put one foot in front of the other.

I've always believed the death ritual is a purposeful way to usher us through the first week of grief so we won't completely fall apart. When someone in the immediate family dies, a normal amount of stress, disorder, and loss occurs.

We are kept busy planning the funeral because there are so many different things that require attention: obituary, casket, religious aspects, funeral service, food, where and when, the list goes on... I dealt with what I had to, but compromised myself in the process. It took months for my heart to catch up.

I no longer cared if my attempts at freedom caused anger in others. I was tired and didn't want to take it anymore. I was desperate to let my past go and heal. I attempted to figure out a checks and balances system. What did I need to do? What did I not have a choice in? What could I take on and what did I need to let go of? I was learning more lessons about detachment, how to let go of what was not mine and become responsible for what was. I knew my trip would be stressful and I would need to deal with all the normal loss of a loved one dying, plus all the excess negativity that plagued my family system. I again couldn't breathe, but was well versed in not being able to do so. Obviously, I didn't sleep. My brain was on overload dealing with all the normal logistics, plus the over-the-top extreme reactions *and* my own feelings. There was also my stepfather's family.

The first shocker came from one of my stepfather's family members a couple of hours after my mother died. They were on their way to the hospital and I asked if they would call me when they got there. The return call was not about the tragedy and sadness over my mother's death, but an insinuation that my mother had *caused her own death* by walking in front of the golf cart.

"Perhaps she was talking on her cell phone," the caller joked. The callousness and chuckle from this person sent me into a tailspin. Nothing was making any sense. I did not want to share

184

this with the family members I was with, but couldn't believe what I had heard. This person's capacity to be so cold and heartless—no kind or warm words expressed, just accusations—sent me further into disbelief.

I knew in every pore of my being that to share the details of this phone conversation would cause an explosion of epic proportions. However, everyone around in those moments could see that I was terribly shaken by the call. They insisted I tell them what was wrong. I briefly held strong, but was too tired to fight their requests. Before I talked about the call, I turned to my friend Barney and stated that my ability to just go home, try to make sense out of what happened, and mourn my mother's death was about to come to an abrupt halt. And I was right: When I relayed what happened, a member of my family went into a rage. I can't blame this person, as the call and the words were horrendous. This family member went into instant action, the kind of action where my needs and voice were once again lost, and would remain so.

I later found out that Jack's family member, the same person who insinuated my mother was responsible for her own death, had driven my stepfather home from the hospital, dropped him off, and left him alone for the night. I thought Jack would either stay at his family's house, or someone would stay with him at his apartment, not leave him alone. I was blown away. Even though he had just killed my mother, I would have never left him by himself. If I'd been in town the night he killed her, I would have stayed with him or found someone to do so. Everything seemed crazy and out of control to me. The next day, Jack's family changed the locks at what had been the home they shared and changed his phone number, no regard for the fact that many would be trying to reach us at the old phone. No one had my new cell number, and I assume many tried to contact me with little success.

185

However, the media—both newspaper and television—had no problem reaching me. The following day, during a long drive to the airport, my cell phone began ringing. It was a reporter asking for a statement because of the circumstances of my mother's death. I had talked to very few people at this point and couldn't grasp why a journalist was calling me. I hung up and called a friend, only to find out my mother's death was on the news and in the papers.

Immediately after landing, my companions and I went to the golf course where she was killed. Her car and purse were still there and needed to be picked up. I wasn't sure why we had to go in that moment, but was not given a choice in the matter. Once there, we decided to walk around. The club was closed, and it was quiet. My mother had been hit on the second hole, so we went and walked the hole to try to make sense of what we had been told about the accident. Jack had told others that she was hidden in bushes when he attempted to drive over to get her. Walking the hole, we saw that there were no blind spots *or* plants. It was pretty much wide open. Nothing he said fit his explanation. It was a challenge to take this scene in, to comprehend all that happened, the whole scene so surreal. Old habits die hard: I went zombie-like, unable to access all that I was feeling.

After the club, we drove to where I would be staying. My cell phone began ringing and once again it was a reporter asking for a statement. A small conversation ensued about how insensitive this reporter was to intrude on my family in this manner. The reporter kept pushing for a statement. I believe my exact words were, "Eat shit and die," or maybe I just thought that.

I'll let my shock and exhaustion take credit.

Once we were at the house, I quickly realized everyone in my family had their own support systems in the way of a significant other, spouse, or children, who were there to help them in the mourning process, someone they could lean on, cry with, and be held by. I had no one. After some phone calls, I asked one of my mother's best friends and a cousin to come be my supportive people. When they arrived, all hell broke loose. Uncontrolled rage ignited over why these two people were at the house. I kept saying they were there for me, but in typical form I was not heard. It was embarrassing and wrong on so many levels. At this, I dove back into my hole and have vague memories of the rest of the evening. These are just some of the events that happened in the first couple of days after she died, and many more continued to happen.

As I slowly began to stand up for myself and use my voice in the coming months, the rage and anger directed toward me kept escalating and felt dangerous. The harder I tried to stop my abuse, the more abused I felt. I would take a step forward in my newfound independence and adult stance. My family circle would balk and attempt sabotage. I would take strides forward in independent thought, pursuing what I wanted to do with my life, how I wanted to do it. They let me know I would fail if I attempted my new direction. At the time I was going through this, I didn't think it was okay to have a goal and fail. I didn't understand that failure is about growth and redefinition. During her life, my mother's anxieties were always there as a roadblock. Now when I struck out and defied my family's expectations, the accusations of failure coming at me only escalated. How dare I try to put up boundaries, to expect respect and create change in the midst of chaos? How selfish of me.

My situation had reached the point where I began to fear for my physical safety, whether real or imagined. I had been afraid since my mother died, very afraid. I was desperately holding on, insisting I was not going to take it anymore. *You no longer have permission to beat me down. I refuse to play.* The night she died, I thought just saying I'd had enough and walking away from the abuse would be simple. That thought was seriously flawed, flawed in ways I intellectually understood, yet was emotionally struggling to comprehend.

Catching up to the reality took three months of walking around numb to the sadness, months of going against what I was feeling so others could have their way. My ability to mourn was postponed by the numbness required to take care of everyone and everything else, for self-protection. Truly feeling the depth of pain at the loss of my mother was put on hold so I could survive. All this while I was still trying to take in and comprehend the fact that she was gone.

I have spent much of my life with my fists up, waiting for the next blow. Here my mother had just been killed, and I didn't even have to wait a minute for the next. It was another tragedy in which I found myself unable to access my feelings and decide what to do, then prevented from being quiet and still to figure it out. In the past, I'd simply go numb. I still can struggle to describe how I feel. In my family, that never mattered; no one ever asked. But I couldn't make this about them or how they did or didn't react. I had to make it about me, about what I needed to heal.

Going numb and trying to care for everyone else just prolonged my grief. The cost I paid by behaving this way took a huge toll on my psyche, health, and spirit. I forgive myself, however, because I know that, due to my family's inability to sit quietly in sadness, my system for taking in truly painful situations was still too weak. I forgive myself because this time was different: I knew I was done.

I wondered how many times I'd had that thought: *I'm done.* How many rock bottoms could I hit? I dealt with the things I had to in the wake of my mother's killing, but was now doing it on my terms. I decided that if my autonomy caused discomfort and anger, so be it. I would let the past go. My mother was dead. I could tell the secrets, which seemed now a final step in my journey.

This was the beginning of my ride in hell.

How devastating that my mother's death delivered freedom. Though this revelation is still enough to bring me to my knees, my understanding is intact.

CHAPTER NINE
THE SILENT KILLERS BEHIND THE BRICK WALL

The saying "You are as sick as your secrets" is part of the work in addictions recovery, and it's true.

THE SILENT KILLERS BEHIND THE BRICK WALL

*"What lies behind us,
And what lies before us
Are tiny matters compared to
What lies within us."*
~ Ralph Waldo Emerson ~

The saying "You are as sick as your secrets" is part of the work in addictions recovery, and it's true. I think back on all the time I spent keeping mine from the outside world, so mortified to let anyone know the destructive details of my life. I had to deal with overcoming the humiliation I was feeling about living and staying in abuse, the shame of which I am sure kept me stuck in it for so long.

I've talked to many people who have kept secrets their whole lives. Some had gotten out of their abusive situations, yet were still afraid to discuss them, simply overwhelmed with the totality of abuse, or unable to be honest with themselves about their pasts. Others don't know how to explain it, the words escaping them each time. Or they are too depleted to give their abusers any responsibility. Many individuals I've spoken with have felt such shame for being abused and were simply too embarrassed to tell. Each time I left these conversations, I wondered why. Why do we keep these secrets?

I realized I was having the same struggle in trying to figure out how to talk about my own. I could no longer explain to myself how and why I continued making excuses, but that is the power of abuse. It is another collective commonality for anyone who has felt this way.

I also wonder how we can change this struggle with feeling we need to keep silent. How do we change our understanding of how to make real and positive impacts on those stuck in these relationships? How do we reach the battered and the brainwashed to give them a language and tools? How do we convey to them that they have nothing to be embarrassed or ashamed of? How do we give ourselves and our children hope for peace? I have so many questions and so much to say about why we keep our secrets, and my experience in finally telling mine, that it has taken me months to get this chapter right. I have done my best to honor and connect with those of you who are still keeping yours so *tight in the bud.*

When my mother was killed, my life changed in an instant. I knew if I did not begin to speak, to shout out my secrets of abuse, I would stay stuck forever. The fear was crippling, but I knew I needed to tell someone, even if they didn't want to hear it. And I knew I would keep telling until I found somebody who would listen. I finally understood my abuse was not something I could fix, and I knew I could not recover from it unless I left. Then there was the very real issue of *how* to tell my secrets and describe what I was feeling.

The night she died, the impact from keeping my secrets escalated, as did the abusive situation I found myself in. I was watching my world fall apart, *again.* On its own, my mother being killed would have been enough trauma, but I was suddenly thrust back into the abuse without a net beneath me, my toolbox unreachable in such insoluble grief. After the funeral, I just wanted to go home to my calm and peaceful mountain life, yet could not leave my hometown. In the aftermath of my mother's killing, I had watched my family fall apart, all while trying to keep my boundaries strong and clear. I refused to take on the placating role of my mother that caused the situation in the first place. I wasn't going to make abuse okay. The only person I could truly take care of was myself, while offering my kindness and compassion to those I loved who were suffering in their own hell. After a period of necessary numbness, I decided it was time for me to start telling.

The day I decided I'd had enough, I sat frozen, contemplating the reality of what I needed to do and the fallout I feared. I spent a restless night thinking about how and to whom I should tell my secrets, and how to write about them. On this particular morning, I woke up exhausted, through with the insanity. My attempts to be done had gone unnoticed, protests unheard by my family since my mother's death. But I was clear, and very scared. It was time. Like Kathy Bates' character in the movie "Fried Green Tomatoes," my **inner Towanda** had had enough. I sat on the couch where I was staying, realizing I didn't know *how* to tell my secrets. Every time I reached a place where I was clear I was through with something, I would feel internally paralyzed and not have a clue how to mobilize the desired changes. My child and I just didn't know what to do, so haunted by memories of our past attempts and rejections.

Holding all my secrets for fear that no one would believe me made me grieve for my child—my little secret keeper, even from me. That morning, though I was scared to shout it out, my ability to keep it all inside was wearing thin, the shame and embarrassment fading away, for I had no more energy for these emotions. It was time for me to deal with one of my biggest blocks and fears, time to let my child know we would not be ignored. *I* would protect her. This was no longer going to be our story. The only player in the circle I cared for was gone, killed. I stayed in the cycle to protect and comfort my mother when her abuse would get bad, though I never felt protected by her.

I was overwhelmed with conflict: I loved and missed my mother with all my heart, while at the same time felt so much bitterness towards her. She had treated me with such anger and disrespect. I was livid she did not leave Jack or tell anyone—except me—how cruel he could be. Though intellectually I knew there was nothing I could have done to convince her to leave, I was emotionally drained and defeated by how hard I had tried. She felt too ashamed and embarrassed to tell, so exploded in a fit of rage every time I said I would. I had spent my entire life being attacked by her, yet she kept her emotional turmoil from everyone but me. If my siblings knew is their story to tell.

I did not want to—I *couldn't*—keep the secrets anymore. The abuse around me was escalating and I began to fear for my physical safety, whether real or imagined, as well as my sanity. I needed to find my voice. That day, I didn't have the answers or the strength to call up my boundaries and tools. I got out of the noise's way, not allowing it to beat me up. I embraced my confusion, pain, and sadness and told myself to feel whatever I needed. I allowed myself the time to search for my strength and courage. Giving myself a pass allowed me to mourn my mother's death and feel the anger I held towards everyone in my cycle. I let myself off the hook, and guess what? It worked. The next day, I felt much stronger and grateful I allowed myself time for confusion and grief.

196

I spent a lifetime thinking that if I stuck with it long enough, stayed quiet and behaved, I could get my abusers to change. I was a good fixer and great listener; my parents turned to me often for their own issues unrelated to the home. Within our family, I worked and worked, yet fixed nothing and kept secrets from the outside world. This confusing dynamic contributed to my staying stuck. If help was offered to me, I didn't trust it. Everything felt unsafe. That's what happens: You keep the secrets of abuse, and once your soul and spirit becomes beaten down, the whole world can feel dangerous.

It is important to understand that this work is very difficult, at times excruciating. Some days overwhelm with their intense emotionality and fear, and we can become crippled when they strike. In those times, it can be impossible to define what we are feeling. I learned there would be days I could not do anything at all, days when I would need to leave the chaos alone and take no action. Letting go for that day did not mean I was losing focus, but giving myself permission to slow down with the knowledge that when I felt better and stronger, I could take a look at the situation. I could address my questions, all of which I understood were based in my fear of the abuse. At least I was finally *asking* the questions. My conviction to tell stood rock-solid.

As I decided to tap into my fears of telling, I needed to come up with a language for myself to understand my eruptions of emotionality. If I separated out the emotions that were keeping me stuck, I could begin the process of forward movement towards sharing my secrets, which I wanted to embrace in a compassionate manner. As I began to separate out my emotions, I realized why it has always been so difficult to answer, "How are you feeling?" That question had always rendered me senseless, never able to explain how I felt. A barrage of everything all at once always overwhelmed me, and still can, the volcanic effect of vomitotus-too-muchus. It could have overwhelmed me back into a numb paralysis, but on this day it did not. I fought the fear of reverting back to my shell of silence. And then I started writing. The more I wrote, the safer I felt to tell the truth.

I stumbled with finding my voice because it didn't turn out like the vision in my head. I've continued learning, falling and getting up, and holding my head high with the conviction that I deserve a peaceful, loving, open life. Most important, I had to keep reminding myself of my worth as well as the value of my story, which is quite taxing when you are being told the opposite.

Infants, in utero and from the first breath they take, are one hundred percent dependent on their mother or primary caretaker for their very survival. Imagine the impact on them if they are born into a family living the secrets of abuse. Secrets interfere with normal developmental growth from the get-go. The infant is born compromised.

Most children do not tell their secrets. When very young, if abuse is happening in their home, it is all they know. They don't understand what abuse is, even though it is affecting their ability to grow and thrive. Their home is a chaotic, scary, and dangerous place. They are frightened, yet don't have the words or sophistication to describe what is happening. Their worlds are full of interruptions during what should be a time of play, exploration, and wonderment.

Since the whole family is living in secrets, so is the young child.

When I was young and throughout high school, I didn't always understand what was happening in my family. It was all I had, all I knew. I didn't even know I had secrets, though I always felt something was off-kilter. I knew the way I felt was different from most of my friends, always in fear over the noise and its unpredictable nature. How could I tell if I didn't know I had something to tell, or the words to explain it? What would I tell? It was my deep, dark hole. I also grew up in an era when you didn't tell, didn't talk about what was going on in your home and kept a good front to the outside world. At least that is how we did it in our family. I believe our neighbors knew what was happening. They watched and heard, but you didn't interfere in other people's lives. It was just the way things were done. There wasn't the understanding about family systems like we have today.

Everyone has memories of their early childhood, whether it was abusive or not. Abuse has so many different shapes and forms. Maybe your abusers made light of their treatment of you. Maybe they threatened you if you told. For many, fear of harm, or threat of death to self, a parent, or pet is very real. An abuser may have complete control over the family and at a very young age you learn not to tell. Threats like, "If you tell anyone, I will kill your mother (or father)," "...I will kill you," "...no one will believe you," "...they will take you away and you will never see us again," "...you'll lose everything."

These threats echo within us as we learn how difficult it is to talk and write about secrets. I woke up thinking about them, those silent killers. I was depleted by the drama and exhausted by trying to figure out how to safely write about the secrets. I decided to let people know I felt I was in danger and hoped they'd reach out to me with kindness and compassion. I was definitely afraid, but knew I had to get past the fear that was keeping me stuck in my situation. I had to confront the wall I had been hiding behind for so long. I had to take the bricks down one at a time.

The first brick was **fear** itself. I had spent so much of my life in constant fear of real or anticipated danger, so to feel scared about what would happen when I started telling was nothing new. And, in reality, it *is* frightening; all my fears were warranted. Thankfully, somewhere deep inside my intuition, I knew I was powerful. I knew my strength was in constant conflict with the control of abuse. I needed to figure out how to comfort my PTS reactions, the physical manifestations of my fear. Living my life waiting for the abuse to occur could no longer be my mode of operation. If I remained afraid of telling, I knew I would never make it out of the hole; my ghosts would follow every step and breath I took. I had many questions to ask myself. First of all, fear of what? Of the unknown? Of my abusive situation escalating when I attempted to leave?

My biggest fear was probably of the **abuser's reaction**. I was also afraid of my family, both immediate and extended, considering me a troublemaker and no longer loving me. I was also hearing repeatedly from my abusers that *I* was the problem. When I first started speaking out after my mother's death, I was beaten down even more. Talking about what I have been through has sent one of my abusers into overdrive. This person is livid I am sharing my experience because they honestly do not believe

200

their behavior is abusive. During a very frightening time, they tried to convince me no one would believe me: I was worthless, stupid, a liar, a cunt. Continuing to talk and tell while being diminished truly tested my grit and determination to be done with abuse. Fearing the trauma of telling my secrets only escalated my own anger. I was angry I had to do the work, livid at the abusers, and enraged at the abuse itself. I knew this time I would need to tell and tell until I found someone who would listen and help. I needed to get rid of the loneliness and the feelings of isolation, even from myself.

I began to understand that I could take my fears with me on my journey; I just couldn't let them have the power to stop me. I knew I would stumble and fall, but had to believe my freedom would give me the will to keep moving forward, no matter how many times I got knocked down. The visions and fantasies of a life free of abuse were tools I tucked into my pocket, as well as awareness of my fears. If I kept them close, I figured, they couldn't snag on anything.

However, in past attempts, I experienced others' **minimization** of my stories of abuse, so that was another brick. Often, the participants of your abuse are known differently to the public, so the thought of not being believed in full only increases the insecurity, fear, and anger. Because my mother was so powerful in the outside world, I had several simultaneous conflicts. Without validation or understanding from outsiders that what I was experiencing was real, I stopped trying to tell long ago. When I would confide in professionals, all of whom knew my mother, my feelings would be diminished and I was told it was not that bad. At least that is what I heard, especially as a child. Perhaps there were those who did understand and tried to help—maybe I wasn't ready to hear or deal.

Having outsiders cut me off made me feel I would always be alone. I'd withdraw back into my secrets and stop trying to tell. It felt like those around me just couldn't understand the enormity of what I was saying, or they didn't want to. I spent much of my life giving up the hope that someone would hear and help me instead of shutting me down and sending me packing to the bottom of my hole. When this happened, even if I'd been working to disassemble the wall, bricks lodged back into place. It's difficult to explain the confusing world of psychological abuse, which for me happened mostly behind closed doors, and I was no longer willing or able to tolerate the reactions of denial.

The minimization happened within my abusive circle, as well. That was the sick dynamic we always played out. They would minimize and I'd accept. I had never before realized that I grew up believing I had to accept the abusive behavior in my family. I didn't tell and suffered in silence, questioning if what was happening to me was abusive. Even as I sat quietly the day I decided to tell my secrets, I still assumed no one would believe me. I couldn't believe I would have to defend my story again, but finally realized I would have to do my internal work myself. I had the education and knowledge and decided to figure out what emotions were behind all the secrets which, on the day my mother was killed, I knew I was done keeping.

When I finally found the strength to tell, many outsiders judged, looked down on me and *did* minimize my words, thoughts, and feelings. Without a witness, verbal and emotional abuse becomes a he-said-she-said situation, or, if the outside gets a glimpse, it doesn't know what to do about it or may not want to deal. For many, it was simply too soon after my mother's death and they were still in shock. What I was telling them was too much to hear, and they retreated from me. This rejection stung. It played down the seriousness of my experience. Some who had never experienced or did not understand true abuse were overwhelmed by my words. Then there were those who simply didn't want to get involved. I was prepared for this as much as I could be, but I don't believe anyone is ever really prepared for rejection, especially when the cost is so high.

When I found those who believed me, I couldn't get them to help. No one I told seemed to understand what I was saying or want to hear it. Some became angry with me, always making excuses for the abusers. I heard things like, "You know them, that's just how they are," and "It's not that bad." I was called whiny and told to get over it. What I heard was that those perpetrating the abuse are just who they are and I should deal with it, somehow accept it, behave, and let it continue. And that's where my anger came in, again. I was disgusted by the outside world's inability to see what was happening. How could they not? I was probably asking the wrong people.

I spent my life feeling **shame and embarrassment** over my situation. In a constant state of fear and trauma, the stigma overpowered everything else in my life. It is embarrassing to admit you are living in abuse once you understand what is happening, yet stay and continue to allow it. Perhaps I felt shame because I couldn't believe I didn't walk away, but couldn't understand why I stayed. One moment I felt in control of myself, and the next I felt trapped. It was an internal war.

I finally comprehended all the years, days, and moments of my life I had missed feeling shame and embarrassment over something for which I was not responsible. I couldn't believe how I—a competent, intelligent, and compassionate person—had become so stuck in my story. Fearful, I could come up with many excuses, ones made in the craziness of abuse, ones that kept me stuck. I had to get to a place where I had nothing to feel embarrassed about. I did not create or cause the abuse. I did not ask for it or accept it. It was inflicted upon me by pros, and before I understood what was happening, I was trapped in it. I had to embrace my conviction that I could not fix it, but only leave. It was time to acknowledge this truth, which broke my heart. It was, and still is, a story that is a no-win for me and I had to figure out how to stop wasting my time.

Betrayal was a heavy brick. I intellectually know that I am not betraying my abusers by telling, but I was betraying myself by continuing to keep it quiet. The outside world needed to see the abuse in order for me to journey away from it, but it could be difficult to remember that I wasn't in the wrong. The abusers seemed to work tirelessly at keeping me feeling like *I* was the abusive one. If I told my secrets, our secrets, I would be hurting them. There would be no chance for them to ever trust me, no chance to "fix."

I stayed with my powerful and publicly admired mother, for example, because I could never have betrayed her by telling our world of secrets. I was fearful it would damage my mother, and I could never have done that to her. Her hold on me was very tight, strengthened by the power and control of abuse. I was so entrenched in the cycle; the feelings of disloyalty would cripple me when I considered telling. Just thinking about it sapped my energy. However, accepting *her* betrayal led me to betray my true, authentic self.

Love is a powerful motivator, and I couldn't let go of my mother. I certainly didn't want, or ask, to be abused, but I couldn't leave. I spent most of my life thinking I could fix my mother and get my father to love me. They had a death grip on me that made it impossible to let go because I didn't have a clue how. Love with abuse is all I ever knew, and I did love them very much. I asked myself if I believed abuse is love. Did I confuse the two? Sadly, *yes*. I had to tell myself abuse was *not* love and finally come to a place where I really believed this. I came up with a mantra for myself: Love shouldn't hurt.

Another brick is **blame.** There were always feelings that the outside world would judge and blame me for the abuse. I was certain others would ask *why* I stayed or assume I wanted to be abused. I even heard that someone at my mother's funeral said, "She chose to stay," of my mother's choice to remain with Jack. Did that mean she was responsible for her own death, or that she deserved to die because she stayed in an emotionally abusive and unsafe relationship? Yet again: what a crock! This is the blame-the-victim mentality. Yes, she could abuse; however, she herself was abused. That only made me more determined to tell.

Blaming the victim and not calling abuse what it is—*abuse*—will shove those being abused further into the closet. Of this I am certain. I believe the laws around verbal and emotional abuse are better, but still need to strengthen. This is a dialogue of which I am passionate to be a part, though I will admit that there are no easy answers. I begin by telling my secrets, even if I then have to insist, yet again, that the invisible abuse I have experienced is real. My hope is that my story can help those of you living in your own psychological abuse.

Another brick represented my own stinky thinking. Another: my vomitotus-too-muchus. Another was my comfort in the discomfort. My denial. All my futile fix-it attempts. The wall had to go.

I began reaching out for help and searching deep within to understand why I stayed in abuse through my adulthood. Beginning to face these questions enabled me to start the process of stepping outside the circle of psychological violence. My boundaries strengthened, one step at a time, as I replenished my spirit and strengthened my heart-mind connection. It had taken me a long time to become brave enough to tell. Finally doing so has created a lot of madness, but this time I have a wonderful protective circle. On the other hand, the reality was that many others abandoned me when I told. I had to make that okay. It is not my problem anymore. There were some who knew and did believe, and that is where I needed to put my energy. What I have learned is that in the beginning I was telling the wrong people. I had to figure out *where* the help was and *then* reach out. I did, and at first I was still overwhelmed, afraid, and very fragile. Once I was heard and validated, my strength and ability to take care of myself grew. My protective circle made me feel secure. I emphatically recommend and cannot emphasize enough that when you get ready to tell your secrets, make sure you have a strong support system around you, made up of people who will believe what you are saying and not question or minimize your feelings and words. If you are met with anything less than what you need—hurtful reactions, loss of friendships—you have the support in place with those who believe what you say. Know that you will lose people you love and care about in the process, but the benefits will be outweighed. After all, what kind of companionship is that?

For many, telling may escalate your already dangerous reality. It can create a very unsafe place for you, especially if you are living with the abusive person. I don't mean to downplay your unsafe, and at times, deadly situation. My goal is not to put those abused in more danger. Each situation is different, so if yours is heightened by physical danger, read this chapter as a starting point and only take action when you are safe. It took some time for me to figure this out, and this is coming from someone in the profession!

It's hard for outsiders who have not experienced and don't understand abuse to believe in the intensity of our realities without thinking we are being overly dramatic. It *is* dramatic and overwhelming. Why would someone make this up? I stand convinced that the *majority* doesn't make this up. Why would I? Why would we? The answer is: We wouldn't. Being believed is what gave me the courage to move forward, and I am grateful to those who have.

The more I was heard, the stronger I became. I had to take a long, hard look at why this was happening. The abuse stayed in the closet; only my family members were a part of it. I have lifelong friends and family who knew things were not good in my home, but had no idea the extent of the problems. What I have learned is that many people already knew. They were watching it happen. In reconnecting with childhood friends, my abusive reality has been validated. One friend told me she stopped coming to my house because members of my family scared her. Another told me her parents wouldn't let her come over. Others confessed they were afraid of my mother. Hearing things I didn't know as a child further validated my experience. It has been empowering. There have been many kind and compassionate people who want to help. For the first time in my life, I am letting outsiders in.

Today I am telling. I will continue to tell. I will no longer live my life in shame, fear, and doubt. I understand the risk I am taking, and I have to be honest: I am still living with fear and working very hard to overcome it. I have no more energy for escalated rage. I could walk away from my wish to connect and give those living in abuse a genuine voice, but I will not. Being paralyzed into submission will never happen to me again. From now on, I decide the choices and direction of my life.

I hope, if nothing else, you see that I am being brutally honest with you as well as with myself. Talk the talk of empowerment and walk the walk towards freedom and know that it will be a difficult journey, but eventually you *will* get it right. I am still learning, talking, and walking. I am not where I want to be yet, but it sure is better. You do not have to be beaten down for existing, or because you are with someone who only knows power and control. That is not a loving, kind, and mutually respectful relationship. Know you are worth love, you can get love, and you can heal from abuse. Put it out there and say it loud. *There is nothing wrong with me. I am being abused.* And remember: Love shouldn't hurt.

TOWANDA!

CHAPTER TEN
LIVE OR DIE

I knew that removing myself from my abusive situation was the only way I could truly feel alive—just as I know how sharing the secrets of my abusive past has value not only for me in my own healing process, but for others who are on their own journeys.

LIVE OR DIE

" How anyone treats you is their responsibility and their karma to answer to; how you react to them is yours.
The way we react is always a personal choice: sometimes it's best to just walk away and leave it behind."
~ Dr. Angela Heppner ~

I knew that removing myself from my abusive situation was the only way I could truly feel alive—just as I know how sharing the secrets of my abusive past has value not only for me in my own healing process, but for others who are on their own journeys. However, this entails the potential intensification of rage from one abuser in particular when I take away his power and control. Since my mother died, I have experienced a face-to-face encounter with this person in which I wondered if I would have the chance to leave the room: I truly thought I could be killed in a blind rage.

The furious barrage was so terrifying, my need to survive kicked into overdrive—between being paralyzed with terror and desperately trying to not escalate the situation. He was spewing his rage, spit flying out in his tirade as he threw my clothes out of the apartment and into the hallway. It tortured my senses, as have all the confrontations I've had of this sort throughout my life. I believed if I made one wrong move, I would die. The anger had taken over—his eyes were black. He couldn't see me through the intensity of his rage. The threats coming at me, quick and straight to my heart, assuring me that how I felt didn't matter, had never mattered. As I watched him spin out of control, screaming at me how worthless I was, I wondered why he was doing this, always wondered why he did this. All I wanted was to have a say, a voice, my own feelings and emotions, yet was being told I didn't have that right. I was once again caught in the web. I felt the same at every episode—demeaned, belittled, and terrorized—but this time something was different. If not my scariest attack ever, it was the moment my denial took a backseat and I had to deal. *Just stay alive.*

Shortly after, I had to attend a meeting with this abuser. As he walked ahead of me down the street talking on a cell phone, I sulked behind, head down, drowning in my humiliation. Footstep after footstep, I wondered why I was allowing this to happen. *Why can't I walk away? Stand up for myself? Why do I allow myself to be treated like I'm worthless? Am I going to remain in the hands of abuse for the rest of my life?* In that moment, I was shocked at my paralyzed inability to walk away and never look back. I simply kept dragging my feet behind, feeling invisible beneath all my shame and humiliation. It was a sobering and painfully honest moment when I realized how I, as an adult, allowed abuse to happen to me. However, any determination to end the madness I had conjured in that moment drained when, after the meeting, he turned toward me, acting nice and funny. Denial crept back in when we decided to buy popcorn and then walked down the street laughing and joking. Two hours earlier I was in fear for my life, yet there I was: grasping onto any show of kindness from this person in my never-ending quest to be loved.

Most frightening to me is the dual personas. Those who abuse often portray different personalities in different venues—whatever best serves their purpose. Uninvolved acquaintances may perceive competent, smart people who have been victimized by those they abuse. The outside world may even assume that the roles in the relationship are reversed. Why would these "abuse victims" be destroying innocent lives with their vicious lies? My fear is finding myself being victimized by the abuser and the world at large as a liar, sick, and out of control. And I know I am not alone with my fears and feelings here.

In past moment of abusive madness, there was a strong pull to just stay in it, endure and be a good little girl (*a good little girl!*) and "earn" love and approval. That is my family heirloom—legacy, if you will—generation after generation of this type of behavior. Keep your mouth shut and don't talk about it. After all, what would the neighbors think? I tried to convince myself I could continue to take the abuse and avoid its spirit-crushing toll. I tried to convince myself I could rise above it, even if it never stopped, and not have it affect me. I tried to convince myself of this because I was so afraid of the abuse and the abusers. I couldn't have been more wrong about that one.

As I've said, regardless of whether I can remember the script of an attack, I can always remember how I felt. Dissociation is a powerful tool, just not a healthy one. Written or recorded attacks such as voicemails don't have to remain secret, but face-to-face abusive episodes, especially if not witnessed, are always more elusive—as I've mentioned, a he-said-she-said. This particular attack was the last I endured in

213

person. This day hit me with a different impact, and I could no longer put myself in these types of dangerous and explosive situations. I just can't do it anymore. With my abusive situation spilling into my outside world after my mother's killing, people began to witness what I had lived my entire life. They were listening to voice messages and reading emails. It was the first time I'd shared so much. As I slowly began to expose my trauma, my supportive circle was concerned and nurturing. In a way, though my personal experience with abuse escalated because I was finally standing up and using my voice, I was almost grateful for the spillover. It was no longer just my word; others were seeing how abuse manifested. They felt the abusers' rage and saw how it was affecting me.

With my mother no longer around to placate the behavior, the claws *really* came out. It wasn't until after her death I began to consider what her presence, in itself, had offered me. Though I never felt directly protected by her, I wondered if the dynamics she'd established had, in the past, insulated me. She may have acted as a buffer, and it wasn't until after she died and I felt fear for my life that I began to wonder if she had had some calming effect on the rest of the participants in our cycle. I now don't think she protected me at all. We were both being abused. I didn't understand that until she was gone.

Meanwhile, the crazy-making reality rocketed to a whole new level. My abusers accused me of spreading lies, which only intensified the abuse coming at me. I was called horrible names in verbal and written threats. The forceful attacks came quick. Despite a mass of confusion on my part, I held on strong, not letting my fear debilitate me in my attempts toward freedom.

Though I was very frightened, I had to move on and away from that type of stinky thinking. I had to deal with my anger at having to do this work. I had to get angry at the anger, accept its reality and figure out how to acknowledge it. I had to jump into it in order to let it go, in order to replace it.

One morning, back in the mountains, I received a vicious voice message. Again, the intensity brutal. This was accompanied by malicious emails I had been receiving since my mother died. These emails and voice message threatened me in every way possible for talking about the abuse. I was called all kinds of hurtful, derogatory names. The onslaught of emails, and especially this voicemail, was quick and effective at sending my PTS reaction into overdrive. It depleted me of all my energy and weakened my stance. I again doubted my ability to stay out of the cyclone. On that morning, I realized that saying "I am done" doesn't mean the abuse—or the abuser—is just going to go away, but I now understood the gravity for my own sanity. I was grateful my friend Barney was with me the morning of the voicemail and got to hear it.

After listening, Barney wanted me to take action, get a restraining order, an attorney to press charges. *Calling the police,* I thought, *for what?* Like my mother's inability to leave with me after my final visit, I was not a point where I could take that leap. At that time, a piece of paper, I believed, would only escalate my abuser's rage and put me in more danger. And it is only a piece of paper—not much comfort or feeling of protection in that. I do understand that restraining orders are crucial in beginning the process of protection for many, but pressing charges for my own psychological abuse seemed futile. The laws concerning that type of abuse for adults don't yet feel protective. They are slowly getting better, but it didn't feel safe that day.

Instead, I went out on my deck frozen with fear, thinking about how my personal abuse was escalating instead of going away, while Barney, stunned by the inhumanity of the voicemail, sat on my couch. This depth of fear was new to me. I did not think it could get any deeper, but it did. The emotional complexity of that moment sent me into a new phase of understanding the fallout. It was then, I thought, I have an understanding of what so many who are battered must feel. I am convinced of this. I kept thinking about how to escape the abuse once and for all and not let it stomp on me anymore. As I stood there looking out over the mountains, a thought came to me I had never had before: *I can't believe I've become one of those women. Have I always been one of those women?*

Then it hit me with clarity as brilliant as the mountains at which I gazed. For the first time ever, I saw myself, and I described who I saw as a victim of abuse. **A victim!** I couldn't stand the thought, let alone the word: *Victim*. My stance is as a victim; my life is lived as a victim. *I am a victim.* I couldn't believe I had lived my life this way. Me, stands-with-fists Debbie, tough and ready for the attack at any given moment, always looking over my shoulder waiting, just waiting.

I was livid. I had never before seen myself in this role. *How do I end this?* Since my mother's death, my attempts to be free had only escalated the rage of the abuse. *What if it never stops and I am haunted by abuse forever, stuck in its cycle of power and control?* It now felt supremely dangerous, even deadly, all because I was finally using my voice and standing up for myself. *How do I calm my spirit*

216

and deal with the PTS reactions, which seem to get worse with each attack? How do you explain to others this crippling fear? I had never felt lonelier in my life.

How do I reach true freedom?

Feeling so violated had severely compromised my ability to simply leave the abuse. In this crippled state, I didn't have the strength to do anything. I was still holding strong that I would not live in abuse anymore, but I was paralyzed by my fears that morning. I was in the most petrifying situation of my life. Leaving abuse is dangerous and scary—the fury coming at me told me so. My fear of the abuser's blind rage ending with my being a corpse sent my emotionality through the roof. My child, awake once again, stood strong, fists tight. It was the moment I knew I was in trouble and needed to reach out for help. I couldn't do it alone anymore. I understood the risk I was taking, my imagined death or freedom, and I took it.

Talk about a moment: I became furious at the power I had given my abusers. I was livid that I had allowed abuse to control my life, constantly giving in to its insane demands in order to stay safe. Here I was, a competent, intelligent, kind woman, and I had hit rock bottom again. I've broken more bones in my ass falling in the hole; it's amazing I can still walk.

And then the most dangerous thought occurred to me: *If this is my life, I'd rather be dead. I will either be free, or die at the hands of abuse trying to get free.* Dead or free, hell of a choice! I wondered if I would be killed trying to escape abuse, or if I would just end my life to have it be over. It was simultaneously a calm and turbulent moment when I thought about the peace of death, the freedom from ever being abused again. That pissed me off. I was not suicidal; I just desperately wanted it to end.

With that, three final questions came to me, the toughest and most sobering ones I've had to ask myself. Consider these the final three questions of the list in the introduction. As you contemplate them, I ask for pure vulnerability and honesty in our collective journey to freedom.

- Do you feel you are at the point where you are either going to get free from the abuse or die trying?
- Does death sound like a better option than going through any more abuse?
- If you have children, are you at the point where you feel your children will be safer if you are dead? (For example, if your spouse in prison for your murder.)

As I thought about my options, I began to understand that for others who are, or were, stuck in the same place, death is real. It happens. To consider death viable is unacceptable for me and for any other person feeling the same way. Dying for freedom is *not* an option. But at the same time, I didn't know what the fallout would be if I shared any more. All I knew was that talking about it was escalating my own personal abusive situation. It didn't stop me from moving forward.

The thought that I could be hurt or even killed were new, though maybe things I feared as a child. It wasn't that I feared being hunted down and killed, but caught in a blind

218

rage attack, dead before the abuser realizes it. At first I thought, with my stands-with-fists tough exterior, I was in control, and my countdown to freedom was in sight. I couldn't have been more wrong. I had to shove my intellect aside and learn this next lesson from my heart. *Brain, move over. You keep getting in my way.* The abuse in my life was not just going to go away with my mother's death. I honestly thought if the abusive players who were left hated me so much, they would be happy to no longer have to deal with me, or have me as a part of their life. I was wrong. The abuse would not let me go, and the stronger I screamed out for freedom, the worse it became.

I already had learned that *I was continuing to choose* to live this life, but now it occurred to me that I *needed* to learn how to be free. When life is built in a subjective world based on someone's opinions rather than facts or evidence, it flies out of control and we live according to someone else. Let me state emphatically that what you feel you are living is exactly correct. It was that way for me ever since my abuse began. I don't think it matters what age you are when abuse starts; it becomes your every-minute reality until you're out.

That morning on my deck, I became more determined to get this conversation about abuse going. I will no longer participate with abuse being tucked away in the closet, especially psychological abuse. And I am sick and tired of abusers being portrayed as victims. We don't have to live like this anymore, but it is our responsibility to ourselves, and our children, to figure out how to make the changes needed for our own survival. We need to increase our level of understanding and education, both personally and publically.

I came in from my deck and called the battered woman's hotline. I decided to reach out for professional guidance, for I knew I could not take the next part of this journey alone. I had reached out for help throughout my life, but it never seemed right. I decided, at fifty-one years old, to give it one more chance. I called a battered women's hotline on a Sunday morning: How's that for divine intervention? And as I waited for a call back, my child stood there with her fists and said, *Fear, go away.* **You ain't the boss of me**.

I received a call back about a half hour later and spent an hour talking to the woman on-call. It was a first step. The next day, I went to talk to a therapist who specializes in abusive relationships. I began to tell my story, explaining my abusers and abusive circumstances as dramatically as I've always wanted to, and guess what? My voice got through. It was the first time in my life that a professional looked at me and said, "Oh, you had one of those mothers" and "Your mother didn't protect you." Someone had just confirmed my lifetime of experiences. It reached my core, authentic self, and I felt heard. My anxiety stilled. Validated, I was able to start healing.

Simply being believed is the greatest gift I ever received.

It took time to let others truly understand the level of my fear and the devastation to my internal being. Many walked away from me, but a handful didn't. I was very proud of myself for taking a stand and moving away from the abuse, but abuse does not go away easily. It still is a slow process. It does not matter what age you are—it is never too late to start your growth, to honor yourself and your experience. Forgiveness begins with self, with healing the self. Again, it's never too late to leave, although—as I'm sure you know—any time you attempt to move out of the circle, its participants will do their best to draw you back in. I don't believe it is a conscious move; it is just the way it works. The players don't want you to point out, leave, or disrupt the destructive behavior. It is the comfort in the discomfort. By leaving the cycle, you are upsetting the already delicate balance of the life they know. When you start to leave, they become angry and hostile and will do everything in their power to pull you back in. They may conceal it with "love," make you feel guilty, threaten you and tell you to behave, or escalate the abusive behavior to make you feel trapped.

I wonder: Why would we want to stay in relationships where we are invisible, have no voice, are hated? Any relationship based on intimidation and verbal and emotional cruelty, any relationship meant to destroy you internally, is a relationship you should leave. Nobody should choose to be in a venomous relationship. As an adult, it is a choice to remain in one.

Think back to the number of times you attempted to fix the abuser through love, begging, walking on eggshells, blaming yourself for the abuse, "if only I had..." Somehow you convinced yourself that this behavior was okay, or somehow your fault. I finally understood: There was nothing I could do to change the past or transform my abusers. The abuse was a perpetual force that remained solid as long as the participants refused to change. Psychological abuse is unfixable if those participating in it do not understand they abuse. My abusers surely didn't, and are still baffled by my claims. However, they will be the first to state how horrible I am. It is narcissism at its core.

If I didn't stop going to those who abused, those who created the madness, I'd never get out. They could not heal my pain or right the wrongs. Staying in the cycle would not allow me to grow or take accountability for my own actions. Growth and healing cannot occur in a volatile circle of abuse. Though the past cannot heal and does not change, what it does give us is the opportunity to learn and grow—if we pay attention. It can help us take back our power and find our voices through our own mistakes. The host of players cannot stop who they are and what they do, especially if they don't think there is anything wrong with their behavior. After all, they are the people who caused the pain in the first place. I had to get to that realization before I was able to start putting the past behind me and move on.

After these episodes, my journey forward became about cutting my ties as completely as possible with the abusers left. I tucked my fear in my pocket and kept marching forward. When attacks would come my way, I needed to figure out how not to give power to the abuse, how to keep my emotional fallout minimal. I wanted to leave the abuse alone, let the abusers keep it. I wanted to learn how to let them explode and implode and *then* leave them be. I understood that there would be intermittent attacks thrown my way, but they could only affect me if I let them. Staying in the volatile abuse cycle makes healing difficult, if not impossible. Every time we step towards independence in our thoughts and desires, the abusive circles are there to pull us back in and tear us down. If you stay in the cycle while doing this work, you must figure out how to separate the abuse from your healing process. I share this because there is no way to heal when you are dealing with someone who is abusive. There is no way to win.

I have spent a life of second-guessing and discounting that which I have always known is true: I have been consistently abused as well as abandoned and neglected. In quiet moments, I understand I was none of those names and accusations being slung my way in the abusers' moments of insanity. I was being abused; I was not the abuse. This fundamental **separation** is one of the most important boundaries to establish. I believe it is a necessary step to separate yourself away from the abuse, leave it as completely as possible, and work toward finding out who you are. No matter what, the abuser should not have power or control over your internal dialogue. The abuser should not have any guidance in your healing, unless it is a lesson you are taking with you. All this time, I realized, I had been trying to gain mastery over living with abuse while I was still *in* the abuse. It overwhelmed me, and I was not getting any better.

Some of you may need to leave the circle completely due to the danger and destructiveness. Some may have children, so complete separation becomes near impossible. Others yet may need to detach for a while to work on your own interpersonal strength, then may be able to re-engage with the members in the circle with clearer boundaries. You are allowed to separate any time you need to, hopefully that does not mean abandoning your children. Each one of you gets to define what leaving will look and feel like. This is about taking care of yourself and defining who *you* are and how *you* will be treated. If the people in your circle cannot treat you by your definition, then why would you want to be in the circle? If you have children, the gift of freedom is priceless. If you stay, you are sending them the message that being abused or abusive is okay.

Even if your choice is to stay with your abuser, take what I've said and sit with it. Begin the process of understanding your internal turmoil. There is no judgment on my part if you choose to stay. Since my mother's death, I now understand that I chose to stay in my abuse until she died. Had she not been killed, I'm not sure I would have left. I will never know. My understanding now is I would have continued to stay because I didn't understand that I had a choice, nor did I have the tools to leave. I can say repeatedly that you can't fix abuse, you can only leave it, but I may have stayed and kept our secrets, even though at the end I was losing energy in participating in the abuse cycle. Her death freed me from my choice to stay. Look at why you are choosing to stay. Perhaps if I had this book, I would have chosen a different path. This is your decision, your journey. Again, no judgment, just questions.

My mother never allowed for a healthy separation process to happen and therefore, I never learned how to be independent. The decision to stay connected to my family and not completely cut the ties as I began my process of **individuation** was mine and mine alone. It was a personal choice, although I don't think it was a conscious one. I knew I could never completely cut off my mother because it would have devastated her. The tie she had on me was so strong and suffocating. I'd always felt very protective of her and her personal demons, in spite of how she treated me. I also knew I was her emotional crutch, and due to her internal insecurities, I worried about her safety. And I did love her. Since her death, I've come to understand how our roles were reversed in many ways. I was her emotional security.

You deserve to be free. To be able to start living a life, to find your own identity that is not wrapped up in abuse. To find your real self who is not being beaten down, or at the effect of the abuse all the time. The true you, who is smart, tough, resilient and wonderful. You deserve to get to know yourself. It has taken me a lifetime to understand that my feeling invisible was valid and it wasn't because I was worthless. When I realized it, I was furious. I had to work hard to switch my *stinky thinking* and feelings away from those who made me feel invisible and find my place in the world where I had a voice and identity, where I mattered. It's a much better world to live in.

As the outside world finally began witnessing the abuse and its impact on me, I entered the most sobering and validating period I've experienced thus far. However, it was also the scariest. It was frighteningly fantastic. I always felt that what I was living was wrong, and I now knew what I was feeling was accurate. With this certainty, I was able to begin my individuation of self. I was finally gaining independence, learning how to navigate the world on my own, learning how to fall down and get back up. Who cares that I was in my early fifties when this happened? I will not feel shame or embarrassment about it. In fact, it has been empowering to nurture my pain, my child's pain, and wrap my arms around her and in doing so, myself. Literally and figuratively, put my arms around myself. What a concept.

When you are so numb to the attacks of cruelty, believe the cruel words, or invisible or real fists are punching, you are in trouble. You are defeated and slowly fading away, and this acceptance of madness needs to stop. Get to a place where you are done with these relationships and learn to take care of yourself. I give you permission to take care of yourself as I give myself the same. Be strong and believe you can do this.

I began to understand that in order to find peace, I had to leave my cycle and those who abused. I reiterate here that this is my story, my experience. This was my personal decision.

225

Everyone's reality of the danger they are in is different. Please note, if your situation is unsafe, make sure you have outside intervention—police, legal, therapeutic, and friends—to support and protect you. Leaving the cycle can be the most dangerous move and, at times, deadly.

As you begin your journey of separation and individuation, you must acknowledge your anger and all your other emotions surrounding being abused. Keep in mind that you are doing it for freedom and peace. Understand that what you have been feeling has carried you through life. If the visuals of my journey and tools fit, use them. If they do not, come up with your own to help guide you in your recovery. This is about self-empowerment and strength. And again, I say this is about a self, defined by you and for you. These are powerful words; *defined by you and for you.* How beautiful! It was not about the abusers or the threats being made, it was about *me and how I reacted* to the threats. If I continued to give the abuse power, it would remain in control. Why would anyone want to try to master abuse when all it does it get in the way, muddying the waters with its senselessness? It is outside our realm of power. The only ones we can control are ourselves: our thoughts, actions, and behaviors. We must figure out how to remove ourselves from the abuse and focus on *us.*

As Maya Angelou says, "You have to forgive to live." For me it's not about forgiving the abuser or the abuse. I interpret this to mean you have to forgive yourself for not being able to change the abuse. I had to find a new path to thrive and give up the wish that the past could have been any different. It can't and it won't, but I needed to embrace it, take from it what worked and leave the rest behind.

I needed to forgive myself. I couldn't change what happened, so I stopped trying. The letting go was my forgiveness. The moving on was the strength. Remember, the abuse is your abuser's problem, not yours. The goal is to keep climbing, no matter how many times you fall.

Now, as I try to let go of what was, the urn of my mother's ashes sits in a closet, wrapped in a blanket made by my best friend, Judi. The urn had sat on top of my fireplace for two years, lovingly surrounded with pictures of her family and friends. I talked to her and stroked her urn in my sadness as I tried to come to terms with her death and our relationship as mother and daughter. At times I screamed at her and wanted to flush her ashes down the toilet in my exhaustion over the abuse, so angry at my abandonment and the work I was devoting to my recovery. I was devastated that—up until her death—this was my life, my existence. And where the *hell* was my father? Mostly, I grieved over her passing and how much I missed her. I experienced every emotion I had in the process of letting go, forgiving, and moving on. I gave myself those two years to heal with her spirit by my side. Allowing myself to feel what I have needed to feel has kept me moving forward. I have begun to let go and find peace instead of anger, though the anger I have felt has been good. It has allowed me to voice and feel what I have denied myself for so long.

899 years of therapy, 100 more to go...

As you begin your journey of separation and individuation, you must acknowledge your anger and all your other emotions surrounding being abused.

CHAPTER ELEVEN
LIFE IS WHAT HAPPENS WHEN YOU'RE TRYING TO WRITE A BOOK

Writing this book has become a journey all its own. Where I am in this moment is not the same place as when I first took pen to paper. Life continued to happen, magical, exasperating, and excruciating events occurred along the way, which have led my journey in a whole new direction.

LIFE IS WHAT HAPPENS WHEN YOU'RE TRYING TO WRITE A BOOK

"The only way out is through."
~ Unknown ~

Writing this book has become a journey all its own. Where I am in this moment is not the same place as when I first took pen to paper. Life continued to happen, magical, exasperating, and excruciating events occurred along the way, which have led my journey in a whole new direction. It has been a personal journey based on empowerment, strength, and defining my life by my rules—along with periods of mind-blowing escalation of abuse in a manner I had never experienced before. Or, it may be that I had never experienced abuse without my mother being alive.

I have called up all my tools and am continuing to use my voice, although I have spent many days in stunned, crippling silence, days when my body literally and figuratively shut down and the slightest movement became impossible. While I am proud of the work I have done since my mother's her death, I do still have moments of complete exhaustion. (And for all you women out there who have gone through, or are going through perimenopause, God is testing my resilience and determination by *gifting* me a traumatic death at the same time I started my change in womanhood. I call it the gift that keeps on giving. I've lovingly termed this my cluster fuck in life's journey. As I look up to the sky and ask "Seriously?" God looks down and says *Yes!)*

When I started writing, I was dealing with the death of my mother, the anger I felt and feel about abuse, and the need to get my story into the world. What happened during this time turned into another component of my personal journey through and out of abuse, because while writing this book, life happened.

One morning, as I sat at my computer, I hit a block. Since the words were not coming to me that day, I decided to go through a box of journals and writings from my life, a box my mother had saved and I found after her death. As I sat reading through stories filled with the sadness of a child lost in the world, I came across something I had written a year after I graduated from high school. In a second, so many questions I've encountered on my road to recovery were answered:

THE LONG AND WINDING ROAD —or— DOWN THE YELLOW BRICK ROAD – 1978 (sic)

There she sat, alone and afraid. It was a beautiful summer type day. Sacha was sitting with her feet dangling in a brilliant blue pond. The reflection she saw in the water was a young child crying. This child looked so sad that it brought tears to Sacha's eyes. But her tears weren't for any young child. The reflection she saw was her own. The tears that fell were her own. Where did it all begin? Why was this happening? When would it all end? All these and so many more emotions were swirling around Sacha like she was being caught by the undertow of a huge wave in this nice peaceful pond. Looking at her reflection, she thought back.

She wanted to die. The thought of life with its vicious games and bicycle cycles made her spit venom. Sacha was tired and was sick of living like a chicken with her head cut off. Her journey down the yellow brick road was leading her nowhere, so she built herself a nice warm cocoon to hide out in. Every time she poked her head out, someone was always there with an ax ready to chop it off. So she withdrew more and more until the pain became so crippling that all her walls came crashing down at once.

So alone, with so much fright this young innocent child desperately prayed for survival. The saddest part about Sacha's life was that she was soon to be twenty. Wisdom and great knowledge were the many assets to which she held on to along with her stuffed monkey she had since she was eight, her best friend. Curious George, her monkey looked like he had just gone through World War III. He looked like Sacha felt. Her life had become so disillusioned that Sacha began to speak through George. What she felt deep down inside George expressed to the world.

When did Sacha realize her emotions were becoming so overwhelming? It was her senior year in high school. Drugs became her great escape to life, requiring a pill just to get out of bed, dope smoking to get her foot out the front door, and speed to get her to class. In between classes, she and her buddies would wander off to the park to indulge in some alcohol drinking and for dessert some joint smoking. For her buddies, that was enough. But for Sacha it was only the beginning.

Sacha's story even goes way beyond the drug scene. Her life battle started even before she was able to realize things were not going right. Nothing was going right.

233

When she was just a small child, Sacha used to lie in bed and have overwhelming fantasies. She was adopted. When she was presented to her parents, an infant wrapped up in her pink washable diapers, the mistake happened. Sacha was given to the lady in bed A and Joey, in his proud blue diapers, was given to the lady in bed B. A bad move on the hospital's part because Sacha's real mother was in bed B. Just because B stands for boy didn't mean they had to give Sacha's real mother the powder blue baby.

Sacha's fantasies grew and grew until she began to feel that these dreams were a reality. When confronting her mother with her feelings, she just smiled and pulled out Sacha's birth certificate. "Sacha Jo Brown, born …" The proof right before her eyes and yet she still didn't believe her mother or any piece of paper. These two people could not possibly be her parents.

Sacha's vivid imagination kept her running wild. The older she got, the more she believed in her fantasies instead of the screwed up reality she was living.

Feeling that she was incapable of achieving much of anything caused Sacha to do poorly in school. She was six years old. Because of this, a tutor was needed to help her with her studies. The first tutor, in a long line of many, was a dear friend of Sacha's family. "Honey," she remembered her mother say, "Mr. Jones is going to help you with your school work. Trust him."

Trust, that word Sacha soon learned to hate. She trusted this man right into her bed. Mr. Jones made a game out of her studies. The game of bed was going to get Sacha an "A" in spelling. So innocent little Sacha trusted this man. After all, her parent's told her to trust him. If he said touching her body would help her pass in school, that's what she let him do. Every time Mr. Jones touched her, her insides cried out in terror. She didn't like the games they played, but went through with them and kept her mouth shut. Her inner pain soon became too much for poor Sacha to handle. It got to a point where she finally refused to see the great Mr. Jones. He was out of her life, but the pain and hatred was locked up tight within her.

Time went on and Sacha continued to do poorly in school. She had no confidence in herself and it showed through in everything that she tried to do, except for sports. Then came the confrontation of all confrontations. She came home from school one day and found her parents in the kitchen. Her sixth sense smelled trouble. The trouble, she knew, was headed towards her. They asked her to sit down and listen to what they had to say. Immediately Sacha turned her inside off button on and sat down with her parents. They wanted her to go back one grade, saying it was for her own good. The catch was that it was her decision.

"It's your decision. It's up to you. We feel it's the best thing for you, but it's your decision. It's your decision. It's your decision. It's up to you." Sacha was in third grade. These thoughts kept running through Sacha's head, so fast and confusing that she ran in to the bathroom and threw up.

Sacha ended up going back a year and her reward was constant ridicule. "Flunker, flunker, Sacha is a flunker." Every day, Sacha ran home from school crying. Why was everyone teasing her so much? Why were they so cruel? These were questions that she had no answers to. The only thing she did know was that her insides were burning and her emotions were an inferno. Her pillow knew of her pain, drenched every night by the tears of a confused frightened child. Why didn't she confide in anyone? Where was the trust? Probably in bed with Mr. Jones.

Every time Sacha wanted to tell her parents what was going on, they were too busy fighting with each other. So Sacha fought with her own emotions, which dug deeper and deeper inside.

As Sacha fought her own battles, her parent's battles led them to do the "in thing." They separated and were finally divorced. This made Sacha happy, because now she would have more time to be with her mother.

Another bomb fell and shattered Sacha's dream of being with her mother. Now instead of all the fighting, her mother was too busy working. She worked and worked and when she came home at night, she was simply too tired to talk.

PART II

She used to bathe in front of me and for the life of me, I can't believe I never saw her penis.

This was when Lisa entered her life. Beautiful wonderful Lisa, her nanny. Sacha worshipped this golden brown goddess. She was tall, elegant and most important, paid attention to lost little Sacha. Now when Sacha was feeling blue, it was Lisa she turned to, not her mother. They sat for hours and hours talking and laughing like children without a care in the world. Lisa made Sacha feel important, like someone special. She told her when she grew up, she was going to be beautiful, a real lady killer.

Lisa allowed Sacha to miss school often. They would walk up and down the streets all day. While they were looking in windows, everyone else was looking at them, or so she made Sacha think so. Men from every end of the city would approach them, talk with them and some Lisa brought home with them.

Lisa introduced young Sacha to drugs. They would sit up and smoke dope until the wee hours of the night. Of course Sacha was always too burnt out to go to school the next day, so she would sleep late and then Lisa would take her for their daily walks and pick up men.

Sacha's body began to change. Her body was tender and sore which frightened her. Lisa would touch her newly developing breasts and caress them softly, for they hurt her the most. Her hands would then wander down Sacha's body to what Lisa called "the pleasure part" of one's body. With her hands between Sacha's legs, she would gently rub. Sacha loved this, for it felt so warm and secure. At night, Sacha found her own hands replacing those of Lisa's and would fall into a delightful sleep...

It appears to me that there is more to this story, yet it ends here, followed by one final page:

...Three men molested; one man/woman.

I sat staring at this sentence. How could I have such vague memories of this? It seemed impossible to me with all my psychotherapeutic work, degreed knowledge, and interpersonal understanding and strength that I would dissociate from these memories from my childhood. In an instant, I found my world of recovery frightening to a once-again fragile heart and spirit. I wanted to scream out my hate for the world for not keeping me safe. The feelings of rage I had toward my parents were immense. My child was abruptly awakened from her peaceful sleep. I didn't want to go back there, but knew I had to.

The memories were gone, just gone, except for one. I had some knowledge of a tutor, as did my mother. He came to our home and I would be tutored behind the closed doors of my bedroom. My mother and I talked about it through the years, but my version pales in comparison to what I now remember actually occurred. And who were the others? Lisa? Not Lisa, my savior who gave me my monkey Curious George when I was a young child. This was the same monkey that I treasured and carried

237

through my life until he disintegrated during my last year in college. I had initially acknowledged her in this book as one of my mentors who brought sunshine into my dark world until I read this story and deleted her from my writings. Not the Lisa whom I trusted with my heart and soul, Lisa who was the man/woman from my list.

Lisa was born a man whose name was David, a woman trapped in a man's body. It was the sixties, and tolerance for this was non-existent. David had a sex change from the waist up and became Lisa. It was her reality in an unforgiving world, and she hid it well. When my mother found out about Lisa, she quickly fired her. I don't think my mother wanted to, but the pressure she got from the outside world to do so outweighed my mother's feelings for Lisa. She even offered Lisa the money to complete her sex change. I found out Lisa had been fired standing in our hallway listening through a bedroom door while my mother told my older sibling. What I got was, "Lisa is gone." I never had a chance to say good-bye to the Lisa who loved, noticed, and was kind to me—the Lisa who I now know molested me.

Learning I had been molested as a child threw me off balance to levels that felt out of control and were very scary. I am compelled to write about my molestations and the impact this knowledge has had on me since I found out about them nine months after my mother was killed. Let me state up front, I have done a lot of my internal work around my abuse and story and am well on the path of recovery. I do not want, in any way, to come across as flippant or callous as I write about what happened. We all get to define our recovery in the way that works best for us.

So here is my disclosure: It is my first open acknowledgment of something I just learned. I will scream it out from the mountaintops and stand tall. *I am a sexual abuse survivor!* There, I said it. I didn't die from the shame of these words; in fact, I feel empowered. I did nothing wrong.

It was time for me, once again, to deal. It does not take away all the work I had done to that point. Perhaps the work was necessary so I could take in the knowledge of my molestations. Perhaps I was ready to deal. Perhaps that wonderful place of self-preservation kept me safe. I realized this was the next step in my journey towards freedom and peace. Even though I was better, there was still more work, more healing, to do. I needed to make that okay for myself. But this time I was not starting all over, even though at that moment it felt that way. I'd come a long way and had the opportunity to get even further away from the darkness.

I began to handle the pain from this revelation with better boundaries, but the process sucked nonetheless. So much began to make sense to me. I was angry—no, livid—that I was back in the hole, having to deal once again with the darkness and the pain. I wondered if my journey would ever end. I'm beginning to understand that the pain can soften, but the journey doesn't end. I now know the journey is called **life.**

As my child woke again from her bed, I hugged her in her pain, and cried with her those fat, sloppy tears. I massaged her fists open and told her I now know one of our biggest secrets. And as we cried together, I realized it was our last step to a complete merging of our spirits, souls and pain. My love and admiration for my child grew that day and I again thanked her for being so brave. I rocked her back to sleep. She needed to rest, for

I know there is more work to come. I was relieved to finally have the answer to such a large missing piece in my story.

Reading those words, taking in the reality of something I have carried somewhere inside of me all these years, I realize that I knew on some level what had happened. At first I sat and tried to access the feelings I had about my molestations, for they are in there somewhere. It was a challenging process. I have very vague memories of some of the events and none of the others, so I don't know exactly who all the molesters were. Perhaps my difficulty in understanding how I felt came from the shut down place of numbness my child has buried deep inside her. To protect me, she closed off the memories somewhere in my psyche: forgotten, hidden away from all, deep in the darkness. My child's furious fists buried all those secrets and memories so she would not disintegrate in her pain, so we could survive. I can only imagine she is filled with shame and frightened by the events so out of her control. Holding her immense sadness in for so many years has caused stiffness in my body that I now understand my drug years momentarily took away.

When I went to college in 1977, my stinky thinking was unrelenting. Drugs and the drug crowd became my way of life. After a particularly bad experience, I woke the next morning and knew I would die if I did not get help. I dropped out of college and returned home to my mother.

Not a good choice..

There were no AA/NA programs yet, or if there were, I did not know about them. I was seeing a psychiatrist and told him how frightened I was about my out-of-control drug use. I wanted to stop the numbing and start dealing with my ghosts. I asked to be placed in a psychiatric hospital. The doctor didn't think it was necessary, but I insisted. I knew I had to go somewhere to protect me from myself, my mother, and the destructive path I was on. I was in the hospital off and on for the next year. It was there I learned about boundaries, choices, and consequences and began building my toolbox. The hospital saved my life. My drug use, however, continued into my early thirties, when I decided to start dealing with all I was feeling.

I did not have to go through being angry at my child for the molestations. I know she did not let them happen, nor was she responsible for them happening. Adults did this to a little girl. They are the ones responsible. I do not sit in judgment of my child nor in shame or embarrassment for her. She has been so bogged down by traumatic memories, a victim of the world at large, horribly violated. And yet she endured. Because she survived, I survived.

Maybe now I can begin to let go of events I am not responsible for and have kept tightly hidden in my repressed memories. I have reached the top of the mountain. It has been a long climb up, but I made it. There is a lot of help available. There are wonderful healing hands and hearts reaching out to all of us. Many have tried to get help, or don't know how to find it.

241

Even being in the professional field of abuse, I did not always know where to turn for help when I really needed it. I learned I was reaching out to many of the wrong people in my search for support, people and professionals who knew my mother and me and didn't believe me, or else minimized. My situation is much like Marilyn Van Derbur, who wrote a compelling book about her experience with sexual abuse, *Miss America by Day*. In her book, she describes her painful journey through her own healing. Her difficulty was that her father, who she states sexually abused her, was so well respected and connected, people could not grasp or believe her abuse happened.

A couple years before I discovered I had been molested, Van Derbur came to my town and spoke about her sexual abuse. At the end of her talk, she asked everyone who had experienced sexual abuse to stand. I wondered if I should stand, thinking I should, but still questioning if I really was a survivor of this type of abuse. It was an intense moment, and afterward I wanted to sit with Marilyn, or reach out to one of the advocate therapists, and talk through what I was thinking. I did nothing, and left feeling dead and empty, Marilyn's book clutched to my side. Now I know why I felt I should have stood.

I had uncovered another missing piece of my spirit, the absence of which contributed to my difficulties in letting go. And it all made sense: my distrust of men, my difficulty with relationships and intimacy, my deep sense of sadness and pain. I was a sexual perpetrator's dream; where were my parents? The discovery of my own sexual abuse shook me to my core and made me realize that due to my neglect, I was a perfect child victim for predatory behavior in the adult world around me. It now becomes part of my history of abuse previously concealed by my **repressed memory.** Even now, with the knowledge of my molestations so new and fresh, I am grateful for this story that has triggered all these memories of abuse. I always had a nagging feeling that something was unhealed and unfinished in my journey. Now I can continue the process with my grit and determination, ever closer to a place of peace.

Survivors of childhood sexual abuse commonly recall an item in the vicinity of the attack instead of the sexual abuse episode itself. If the attacks occurred in the bathroom, they may remember something like a shower curtain, not the actual violation. The focus is zeroed in on one thing as a way to not be emotionally present for the abusive encounter. In my own experience of being sexually abused, I have always had a severe physical and emotional reaction to a certain type of buttoned down T-shirt. When I see someone wearing this style shirt, I get an emotional kick in the stomach and feel physically sick. I once even asked a date to change his shirt when he showed up wearing one. (Let's just says there was no next date.) I never knew why I reacted this way. Upon learning about my own sexual molestations, I now understand it better.

Perhaps memories from our pasts need to come up in a natural progression, in bits and pieces, so the work to be done feels safe. Maybe I needed to find my journals that described my molestations after my mother died. If she were alive, I may have been buried back into shame and the darkness due to her anxieties, guilt, and inability to acknowledge my pain. Perhaps I needed her to be dead so I could be my own mother.

Hell, up until now I feel like I've been a very good mother to my child in our joint-healing process. So it is now time for me to go back there, weed through all the muck to come out the other side. And with everything I have learned about healing and a lifetime of experience with abuse—some created by me, some by the outside forces of my perpetrators—I heal some more.

Let me be very honest with you. I'd like to deny my molestations, my mother's killing, and the next step in my journey. I'd like to go back to my fluffy bed in the sky with my child, animals, down comforter and just sleep. Sleep away the sadness, the shame, the fear and rage and anger. Keep away the abuse. And that is a choice we all have to make. You can put off what it is you know you need to do, but I guarantee you it will come back, and when it does, it will do so with a vengeance. The longer you put off dealing, the bigger your conflicts will become, or if you choose denial, the unconscious effects will haunt without you knowing why. Bring it up, deal with it, or else it will never go away. You will never forget what happened, but you can get to a place where your story no longer controls your life. Do it for yourself and future generations. And if you are pissed like me, use my fists, for determination, to help guide you.

At times I have wanted to shred this book, stop the despair and go back to my life of dissociation and denial, for there is brilliance in these reactions, the not-knowing what we know. Making sense out of the senseless is draining. My understanding into the world of abuse has just taken on a new path, for I now get to look at one more abuse in a lifetime of its forms.

My needing to deal with the pain and shame begins again, only this time I am stronger. I will continue my journey because I want to let it go and be done with events I had nothing to do with.

This journey is mine. Each one of you has your own to navigate, defined by you and for you. It is those powerful words that will allow you to take back control. My heart is with each and every one of you who has gone through any type of abuse. I share this with you because you need to know how difficult this work is. Each one of us will have a different journey and the processes of discovery and recovery will vary.

I say this with pride: The worst of my suffering is over. I now get to bring up all that remains and is unconscious so I can move forward toward the light. My work continues, but I am on a different street, tool belt on, ready to embrace my peace of mind and spirit. I am moving forward and I am free. There will still be days when I fall, but I will get up dust myself off and continue my forward movement. It is not perfect, but life is not perfect for anyone. Because now I know: Life is what happened while I was writing this book. I am a work in progress and, for the moment, I will just breathe. How simple.

I say this with pride: The worst of my suffering is over. I now get to bring up all that remains and is unconscious so I can move forward toward the light.

EPILOGUE
KNOWING BETTER, DOING BETTER

When you decide to leave the cycle of abuse and gain autonomy, some things may get worse before they get better. It terrifies and enrages the abusers to lose their power and control. The decision to leave the cycle is a personal one for each of us.

KNOWING BETTER, DOING BETTER: ONE STEP AT A TIME

"Never be bullied into silence. Never allow yourself to be made a victim.
Accept no one's definition of your life; define yourself."
~ Harvey Fierstein ~

I chose to walk away from the abuse, to leave behind forces over which I have no control, abandon the dark mess and move towards the light of my own salvation. I will come to terms with the changes I need to make. Rearrange my focus. Find my inner peace. Stumble and continue to climb out of the hole. Grow some more from the inside. Find my heart, love and nurture all that is me. I will keep my fists unclenched.

There has been huge fallout from my mother's death. Some have considered me a narcissistic monster for finding freedom, but I've been called worse. Many are exhausted by my journey, and I understand. I'm exhausted as well at how hard I have fought and how long this is taking. I've lost many, yet most have been loving cheerleaders of support in my quest toward freedom from cyclical emotional and verbal assault. There are those who care. I no longer need to be around people who tear me down, no longer needed to dance in anger. I know my journey towards peaceful quiet and the ability to breathe is working. My tools are stronger and my boundaries clearer and I accept there is more I have to endure in my quest for freedom. I will no longer let abuse beat me down and will keep marching forward, never allowing my goals out of sight. I now have an end date: healing from my mother's death and learning to live life to its fullest. It has been a bittersweet journey, and as I grow, I will do it with grace, wisdom, dignity, integrity, understanding, and compassion. That is my authentic self.

That is my story, but this book is not as much about my history as it is helping others find their freedom through their own voices. As I've stated at the beginning, we all have our stories; it is our commonality. The work towards freedom becomes about what we do with them. That is where my focus remains. Perhaps my journey was to write this book, have my words published with the hope that what I have to say is significant to those in their own terror and pain. Perhaps my words give evidence to events in my life that happened and that, until now, I shared with few. All my secrets of a lifetime. I am positive of this book's value, written to give you, the reader, your own voice and validation. At the core, we all have the same story, just different adaptations.

When you decide to leave the cycle of abuse and gain autonomy, some things may get worse before they get better. It terrifies and enrages the abusers to lose their power and control. The decision to leave the cycle is a personal one for each of us. There are many levels of the many types of abuse you may be experiencing, as well as levels of danger you may be putting yourself and your children in by attempting to leave. The type of abuse and the way it is perpetrated is also different for each of us, along with the way we have been hurt and internalized it. Even acknowledging we are being abused can be difficult without making excuses about why it is happening. It can be very scary; for some, it is crippling and may be what keeps so many stuck inside. Furthermore, death or the threat of death may be very real. You may be so beaten down that you don't have a clue how to get out, or you no longer feel you have a choice. Maybe you never knew you had one. You may not feel able to survive without the abuser's financial support. You may still be so emotionally attached to your abuser that thoughts of leaving don't even exist; we *can* feel real love for our abusers. We love the person, not the behavior. Many of us don't know how to deal with our broken selves, including the abusers. But it is their responsibility to fix themselves, not yours. If you do not leave, you have chosen—like my mother chose—to give your life to abuse. Again, I do not sit in judgment with those of you who choose to stay. I understand the difficulty with that reality because I also chose to stay for my mother. Another hope is that professionals begin to understand the crushing decision of making the leap of faith to leave. There is always a high cost. For the reader, all I encourage is that you ask yourself *why*.

One day I was talking with my therapist when she asked, **"What are you saying goodbye to?"** That has been an important question, because saying goodbye to those both living and dead has been a big part of my journey. Yet I now understand the cost is too high to keep them in my life, heart, and spirit. I've been dealing with a lifetime of immense anger, furious with two parents who did not only abuse, but did not protect me from other abusers in my life. I've had to come to terms with all my questions: What did I do to deserve this life? Why didn't my parents care? Did they ever love me? All of these now seem so futile, for I will never have answers to these questions my little girl has clutched so tightly for years.

As my verbal and emotional abuse continues, I feel enormous sadness, because taking care of myself means the "family" I knew is gone. It meant fracturing a family which, for me, existed only because of my mother. This breaks my heart, but the need for freedom overpowers the grief. It's now a different dynamic than what held us together for all those years. This needs to happen if I am truly to be happy.

Saying goodbye to the family you were born to, or married into, or may be in relationship with, is excruciating. It is not an easy choice to let go of all you knew, of what was, of who you were. My situation makes me an orphan in my own story. The years upon years' worth of tears I have stuffed away are, bit by bit, filtering out. During a recent session with my therapist, I allowed my vulnerability to the surface. I used an entire tissue during that session to wipe away the visible tears running down my cheeks. It was a time for me to celebrate because I am finally letting go, one tear at a time. Single piece of tissue used, 998 to go. I am very proud I am finally trusting the healing process and letting others inside to see the pain I feel. I will nurture myself until I can release completely.

As a therapist working with survivors, there always came a point when we talk about how scary it is going internally to the pain of abuse. Many feel like if they tap into that scary place, they will die. I was able to understand because I felt the same panic of being engulfed by the intense emotionality and fear. I had always felt that if I went in, it would be so overwhelming that I would die in the process. I'm not sure if it is an actual physical death I feared or an emotional death. But it is scary and always has been.

I am dealing with the anger I have held so I can let it go and continue to move on. It is hard, for my rage has been a way of life, but I know that stance blocks me from moving forward and accessing my inner self. At first, when I'd try to tap into the pain, I would just stick a toe into it and immediately recoil, what I felt too overwhelming. I continued to stick that toe in the pool until I could keep it in the pain. Once the toe was in, I was able to start accessing more of my spirit and what I was feeling to stay in the moment. I've started the process of embracing my feelings instead of running from them. It's hard, but I am slowly getting better. Eventually I will be able to dive in head first.

As I discussed my clients' fears with them, I explained what I believe is a two-fold process. I told them a part of them would die a metaphorical death. The therapeutic work was about letting go and being done with the abuse, being reborn. Closing one door, then opening and walking through another: Freedom. My job was to go in with them and not let them become engulfed or overwhelmed by gently guiding them in the process. The journey would begin.

I found that I had to take my own words and apply them to myself: go back in, die again, and become reborn. I love the symmetry of this, but have always feared the reality. Strengthening the heart-mind connection is difficult, and accessing the totality of a lifetime of sorrow is terrifying. Thinking of the rage locked inside me overwhelms my senses with a sadness that brings me to my knees once again. If I didn't do this work, I would never recover, because I understood and had to learn again it was no longer about my abusers, it is about me: Me as the common denominator.

I would let the abusive behavior belong to the abusers. I would let the abusers deal with their demons and I would stay out of the way. When it crossed over to me, I would understand the attacks have absolutely nothing to do with me. I would do my best to leave it alone and not get tangled in its ugly dance while I learned how to take care of myself. Still afraid, I knew it would take strength to let go of what was and move toward what is. I knew that I had to follow my own advice. What a concept. *Whodathunk*?!

Just waiting around for the next blow would *not* be my reality. I would deal with the rage and anger I have towards two parents who watched a little girl drown. I would figure out how to let my abusers implode and explode on their own, and when the attacks come my way I would no longer be rendered senseless. If I was, I would have a support team around me to work through the pain.

253

One day while on a riverside hike, I stopped to sit on a large rock. It was spring, and as the snow melted away from the mountaintops, the rapid water movement and sounds of nature all around gave me a moment to take pause, breathe, and reflect. Sitting on this rock, the water rushing towards me, I began another vision of my life defined by me, for me. I came up with the following commandments for self. The most beautiful part about them is that I decide. They will grow, change, and flourish as I continue to move forward. It is a beginning. I urge you to make your own commandments, and feel free to take any from my list that may fit.

MY COMMANDMENTS FOR SELF

- I shall hold my head high and embrace my voice with compassion, dignity, and strength, while quieting my spirit and calming my heart as I continue to grow. I will do this with kindness, wisdom, and understanding.
- I shall hold onto the belief that life is a learning experience and always stay true to my growth and direction, even when I fall from time to time.
- I shall be mindful of my triggers of a lifetime so when they fire I can work on quieting and calming my spirit while opening my heart to new ways of coping.
- I shall honor my fists, my determination for forward movement, and shall dedicate my life to helping others on the same journey.
- I will keep my sense of humor, always.
- I will stop trying to fix the uncontrollable, that which I cannot change.
- I will no longer let my fear dictate my fate.
- I will continue to bandage my own knees.
- I will use my voice for strength and healing.

- I will continue to dance in the rain and laugh from the belly.
- I shall give my compassion and understanding to those in the world of my mother and family if they respond to my voice with rage, anger, disbelief, or accusations. I will understand they have their own story, memories, and belief systems. I will accept their realities as their truths and give them compassion and understanding to their reactions as I let go and move on. I will allow them their own voices. This one, I understand, will take strength and truly test my resiliency.

YOU HAVE THE RIGHT...

- ...to respect.
- ...to change your mindset and believe you are worth it.
- ...to empower yourself to live, as an adult, a life defined by you.
- ...to be nurtured and supported by those in your intimate relationships.
- ...to make some noise, stamp your feet, and "mess up" your circle to stop the abuse.
- ... to set goals and change your situation, to stick with it no matter how hard the challenge.
- ...to be a better role model for your children so they can learn to make safe choices, communicate effectively, and have the tools to survive in the world.
- ...to feel good about yourself with the knowledge that you are not a bad person, and you are allowed to be imperfect without being abused when you make a mistake.
- ...to believe that you are more than an abuse victim or survivor, to believe you are more than what your abuser says.

- ...to go into the world and discover not only what your talents are, but who *you* are, a valuable and important individual in our society.
- ...to dance in the rain and learn to laugh from the belly.
- ...most importantly, to embrace a life without cruelty, to live in peace and experience real love away from the fear of being abused. You have the right to be free, to be seen, to be heard.

TAKING STEPS TO GET OUT OF ABUSE

- Turn to that one or two trusted friends and tell them what is happening, even if it is someone you have not been close to in a while (maybe because of the abuse). Chances are they may already know, feel powerless to help, and are just waiting for you to reach out. Perhaps they *will* be there to cushion your fall. Keep looking for that kind spirit, even if some reject you. Help is out there. It has taken me years to learn how to find compassion and understanding, but, as I've said, I was asking the wrong people. Use your intuition, and when others react in ways out of your control, if you feel rejected by their response, remember to keep persisting until someone believes. Rejection never feels good, but it is reality and quite understandable. After all, this life has been overwhelming you for what I'm sure seems like forever. At the same time, you will also be amazed at the people who do come forward and open up their hearts and hands. You'll be surprised at the commonalities you'll find. Sometimes you will find compassion in the last person you ever expected to reach out to you with such tenderness.

- Find a support group in your area. I have given a list of sources to reach out to at the end of the book. There is power in numbers and safety in being part of a group that truly understands all the sticky symptoms of abusive situations. They are there to help validate, to listen and strengthen you. You will feel empowered by being able to help your peers, your village, your people. There are also mental health centers that can offer help, support, and therapeutic services. If you don't like one group, therapist, or service, keep looking until you find something that works for you. Clock's ticking.

Abuse is not mine alone. It happens to neighbors, friends, co-workers, and relatives. It happens all over the world. I happened upon both my editors. The first grew up in abuse and initially took a different path of recovery. When we came together as a writing team, she found herself swept up again in her own personal family drama. Editing the book as she dealt with her personal situation helped her strengthen her own tools in dealing with abuse. It was wonderful to watch her as she grew, as we grew together. The second was a young woman in graduate school who almost married her abuser. She came from a wonderful family, and yet found herself in abuse before she understood what was happening. The relationship was over when we came together, but the memories still haunted her. As she read my book, her own internal struggles where triggered and we spent time working through her trauma as we edited. Both experiences made me understand the need for this conversation.

Everyone's experience of abuse—its types, severity, and frequency—is different. It does not matter the degree to which your abuse is or was inflicted; it is all abuse. No one story is more important than another. The experience of abuse is what binds us. Everyone living in it has his and her own stories to tell. Everyone has a different take, different injuries, a different history. I have come far in my journey towards freedom from abuse and its impact on my life. It has never been easy and I continue to work on myself every day. Forward movement in health, happiness, freedom, and peace has been and will remain my ultimate commitment to self. This is my history, my reality, and my story. It is only mine, and the only one that matters to me in the end. I have earned the right to my own health and sanity, for if I don't take care of myself, no one else will.

Here is my wish and hope for you, the reader: If my words have resonated, stirred up, or helped you begin your own journey away from abuse, take my story and hold your head up high as you move through your own dark reality towards the light of peace. The journey is to have a voice, to be seen, loved, accepted, nourished, and hugged. The goal is to be happy and free. So please take my hand which I extend to you, open and ready to hold as you take your journey. My heart, spirit, and compassion are with all of you. I'm on the other side of abuse, unpacking my boxes. There is room for all of you to move to my new street.

LETTER TO MOM

I am grateful you are finally at peace. I know you did your best. I know you loved and cared. I know you were the best mother you could be, even though I still struggle to understand it. I am devastated by your loss and I will grow and learn from our relationship.

LETTER TO MY MOM

Dear Mom,

As I sit here writing this book, talking with your many friends about the impact you had on them, and healing to a settled place over your death, I felt compelled to write you this letter…to my Mom.

I've been overwhelmed by the circumstances of your death. I've been overwhelmed coming to terms with the history we shared. I've been saddened by how to encompass our relationship of mother and daughter and to bring closure to its existence. It was a hell of a ride. At times wonderful, magical, and exhilarating. At others: bumpy, chaotic, and heart-wrenching. I want to remember you with grace, acceptance, love, compassion, and kindness. I want to carry your memory with me always. And I feel I can do that since I am letting go of the pain and heartache. I can do that, for we were all "at the effect" of heartache. We were all "at the effect" of pain. We were all trying to survive circumstances out of our control for so long. And I am letting go "one step at a time."

I find comfort in knowing you are finally at peace. I believe your fears and anxieties have been laid to rest. I'm finding comfort having your ashes with me as I heal from the pain of your loss. I talk to you, stroke your urn with love and rage as I learn to let go of my anger and what was. At first your presence

261

was everywhere and at times Bo saw your spirit flying around. I'd tell him it's Baba and he would wag his little tail in excitement as he ran around the house looking for you. But most of all, I am working very hard to move forward.

I think what I will miss the most is the thing I've always hated the most, your energy. It was that energy that kept you away from home, kept you away from mothering, and kept you away from me. But as an adult, I have come to understand your need to run. And run you did, always with vigor and excitement. I know why you ran when we were children, so overwhelmed with our need for you and your inability to handle the pain of what the divorce did to you and us kids. Dad left you alone. He abandoned us all. You were left with small children and he never looked back. His indifferent interference, our need for him in our lives and the anger you must have felt probably made for many sleepless nights in your life. Your fear of how you would raise young children, how you would pay for us and how you would survive I know overwhelmed. I didn't know then, but I know now.

My heart sobs for your sadness during those times. My heart sobs for the fear and loneliness you must have felt and carried with you. My heart screams that you were forced to make the choices you did. And I was left shattered in the aftermath. I know you suffered because of this. It has taken me a long time not to blame you for what I felt was your indifference. It is taking me a long time to heal from the pain of loneliness and feeling worthless in a chaotic and dramatic world. It's interesting to me how the parent that stays gets all the anger and rage. Maybe it's because even though you were not there, I always knew you would never completely abandon. That in itself was always confusing: there, but not there. It has taken me a long time to let go of the anger and move towards complete forgiveness. I am still working on this.

But I am. I am getting through the pain and growing up. It has allowed me to separate out and find the goodness and magic that was you. I've always been amazed by your thirst for all that is life. I've always been amazed at your power to touch the masses. I've loved and am proud of how you cared and worked tirelessly for causes that touched your heart. And you have left so many behind who are devastated by your death and miss you on a daily basis. You were loved by so many even though you didn't know it. It's what made you so special to all, your unassuming nature and down to earth sensibilities. I've never met anyone with more mothers, sisters, brothers and friends. Not bad for an only child.

I know some will feel like I betrayed you by writing this book. Most have given me loving support and words of empowerment as I walk through the journey of letting go. I am certain of how proud you are of me and my wish to help and make a difference for others living a life of pain and abuse, because that is what you were all about, making a difference in people's lives. If this book does what I hope it does, many will leave their abusive situation and move to a life that has purpose, hope, health and peace. My hope is that your death will save many lives. No matter what anyone thinks, I know you are looking down and are proud of this book because secrets don't matter to you anymore.

I am grateful you are finally at peace. I know you did your best. I know you loved and cared. I know you were the best mother you could be, even though I still struggle to understand it. I am devastated by your loss and I will grow and learn from our relationship.

Despite everything, in the end, I loved you very much. My sadness at your loss is insurmountable. My forgiveness to myself and you for not being able to stop the abuse is complete. My gratitude for the good is intact, and the knowledge that I couldn't fix or change anything other than myself is understood.

You rocked my world: the good, the bad, and the ugly. May you rest in peace.

ABOUT THE AUTHOR

 Debbie Zoub, MSW, is a clinical social worker and a survivor of abuse. She has spent much of her twenty five year career working with all types of abuse both as a therapist and caseworker. Her professional and personal understanding of living a life in abuse is what created this book.

I invite you, the reader, to join me in this journey to leave abuse behind so together as a community all can gain empowerment through each other.

DEBBIE'S INVITATION

I use the title and term *Stands with Fists* not in violence but in grit and determination to be done living a life in abuse. I wrote this book with the goal of giving you, the reader, a language and a voice in your own abuse. It is a raw book about the journey out of abuse without having all the answers.

As I am trying to leave my abusive past behind, I truly understand why so many women, men and children keep the secrets of abuse behind closed doors. I understand this because my own journey continues and each time I get knocked down, I wonder why I should bother. It often feels like a no-win situation and that it will never end for me. But it is with my tenacity that I continue on my own journey and offer help to those on theirs. It is my contention that when you grow up in abuse, you don't always know what you are living... is abuse. As I grew, I became aware of my situation. I knew that being yelled at, put down, invalidated and made to feel worthless and always wrong was not right. I knew that my spirit was being crushed and my ability to grow was being beaten down. I knew for most of my life that I was in trouble. But, I didn't have a clue what to do about it. So, I fell apart and lived that way through most of my life. That was until I screamed, "I've had enough." I had enough of others defining who I was, enough of giving my power away to abuse and those who abused. I was finished. That was when my journey towards a life away from abuse began. I now honestly acknowledge that the journey away from abuse is exhausting hard work, at times excruciating and it has taken me

267

time to find a peaceful way of life. I am getting there and at times, still getting there.

I invite you, the reader, to join me in this journey to leave abuse behind so together, as a community, all of us can gain empowerment through each other. It does not matter what type of abuse you have experienced: physical, sexual, verbal, emotional or neglect. It is all abuse and it takes a toll.

So, today I start the conversation by sincerely spreading the message in this book along with my care and compassion. I also extend this invitation to all of you. I am DETERMINED NOW to change how the world views abuse. The journey out of abuse is hard; the freedom from abuse is priceless.

You can contact me via email at Standswithfists333@yahoo.com.

Debbie

APPENDIX

"The most common way people give up their power is by thinking they don't have any."
~ Alice Walker ~

Diagnostic Fallout from Psychological Abuse

This Appendix is devoted to breaking down the key words and phrases of this book that bear repeating as well as helping you make sense of how your mind and body may be responding to abuse. There are many psychotherapeutic diagnoses given to those who are being or were abused and seek professional help. You may be feeling numerous physical conditions due to your mind's inability to deal with your abusive circumstances. These behaviors have helped guide you through your survival; they have kept you alive. I believe we have developed brilliant reactions, not disorders, to the abuse being inflicted upon us. For myself, I needed to put what I knew professionally into terms that make more sense to me to lift the heaviness of diagnostic criteria. It helped me feel not-so-crazy. Since I love words, I came up with a language I could understand, using humor whenever possible.

Pick any of the realities listed below that fit your situation as a way to start defining your abuse for yourself, to articulate—to yourself and your support system—how you feel and have felt. You may even have some to add that are not listed and fit your own personal experience. Your feelings cannot be disputed. Remember, they are warning you to do something about your situation. You are much stronger than you think, and in control of your destiny.

If anything below resonates with you, and even if you add some not listed, you have a choice to make. You have to decide if you are done with abuse. You may never be able to be completely away from your abuse, especially if you have children, but the amount of power it has over your mind, body, and spirit can change for the better. I write this not to diagnose anyone with any type of disorder, but because having a language to describe what you are feeling and going through is crucial. Again, I strongly believe you are not a disorder, but reacting to and surviving abuse. Your reactions have become your strength and power, your ability to survive. There is brilliance in understanding and using these emotional realities so you can find your tools and begin the recovery process out and away from abuse. Now is time to do something different and healthier.

Educate yourself about what a healthy relationship looks like to validate that your situation is unhealthy. It is a step toward learning how to find the tools you need to help you make better choices. In learning, know that you have value, are smart, and have incredible survival skills. It is now time to use those tools and skills for health and happiness. You deserve to be in relationships that bring out your best, ones that enhance your sense of self-worth and, most importantly, ones that are safe.

Again, this section is not intended to diagnose any medical or psychological condition. I am not a doctor, and if you are experiencing somatic, physiological (interfering with normal healthy functioning), and/or psychological (mental or emotional) symptoms, *they are real.* You should always address these symptoms with appropriate medical and psychological intervention. And remember: no matter what your abuser may say, you are not sick or crazy; you are surviving.

ABANDONMENT FEARS

Every relationship I entered started out solid and strong. Things would be playful and fun. However, as each relationship progressed, my fear of abandonment would take hold. As my fear grew, I would unconsciously become angry and hostile, displacing the anger and distrust I had towards my father on my other relationships. I believed the men, and people in general, were abandoning me, even if there was no evidence to support my fears. My behavior, due to these beliefs, created a pattern that ended with people I cared for leaving me. This self-fulfilling prophecy counteracted everything I wanted and needed: to be loved in a mutually satisfying relationship.

ABUSE

n. improper use; *v.* to misuse
With this knowledge, the word "abuse" becomes quite transparent. Love shouldn't hurt.

ABUSIVE REALITY

Abusers rarely abuse one hundred percent of the time, creating a cycle from abuse to calm and back again. Sometimes, the calm can be almost blissful—or perhaps this is just comparatively speaking. We tend to hold on to any tender gesture from our abusers like they are the generous gifts. However, this kindness never lasts long, and we continue searching for it—like addicts. In the good moments, I desperately wanted to believe that all was finally good with the world, though my history told me it was not. During good times, we may feel heard and recognized as individuals, only to have the supposed understanding disregarded in the next encounter. This was the delicate dance of abuse I was always trying to perfect as it slowly instilled my doubt in my perception of reality. *See: Addiction, Crazy-Making Reality*

ABUSE TURNED INWARD

Our critical internal voices act as a continuation of the psychological abuse we endure. For me, this was my constant internal conversation, the obsessive thought reaction confirming what the abusers were always telling me, that I was worthless and stupid. This voice kept me stuck in the abuse by reinforcing it, agreeing with my abusers and validating their behavior. These self-destructive thoughts were always in conflict with my feelings of self-worth. I knew I wasn't worthless, but I also didn't know *what* I was. It was my own internal double bind; it made me feel crazy.

It has always amazed me how we humans are so willing to hold on tightly to the negative stuff. We allow it to ring loudly in our heads and keep us from seeing the beauty—or potential for beauty—of our world. I had to stop focusing on the negative and stop giving power to those who couldn't, or didn't want to, hear me. I had to embrace what was good. *See: Obsessive reaction, Stinky thinking*

ADDICTION

Abusive relationships of all kinds—and perhaps especially psychological abuse, which punctuates most physically abusive relationships—have properties as addictive as any substance. We crave the "fix" we feel during the good, calm times of the abuse cycle. This is why addiction mottos and catchphrases from programs such as Alcoholics Anonymous have been such helpful tools for me in my recovery process. They also may come in handy if drugs or alcohol are or have ever been a means of escape for you. *See: Escapism*

You are as sick as your secrets. This was the core of my learning. I didn't want to—couldn't, *wouldn't*—keep the secrets anymore. Keeping them was sickening my body, mind, and spirit.

Letting go of my secrets was the toughest and best gift I ever gave myself.

One step at a time: This is where you start, even if you don't yet know what direction to go. You can pivot, and maybe even twirl. So long as you're listening to your intuition and *truly following* it, you'll be able to keep moving forward. When you're tuned in, you'll feel pulled forward as if by a magnet. I still use this motto when overwhelmed to keep moving forward, no matter how difficult it can be. We must give ourselves permission to make mistakes, fumble, fall backwards, and embrace every step forward until the nagging discomfort becomes a thing of the past. When the abuse rears its ugly head, you move away from it and any of your own negative reactions. Every step away is a step closer.

I will fake it until I make it. This saying was very useful when I first began my journey, scared by not having a clue what to do. Learning that it was okay to fake it until I learned what I wanted to get rid of and what to keep helped calm me until I strengthened my definition of self.

Give it up to a higher power. Even though I still struggle with what my higher power *is*, I find relief when I release the events that are out of my control, send my thoughts and feelings out to the universe. The universe can have it; I sure as hell don't want *it* anymore.

ANXIETY

Anxiety affects thought process and the cognitive thinking ability, and takes a real toll on the body with somatic reactions such as a rapid heartbeat, panic attacks, stomachaches or digestive issues, headaches and migraines, breathing issues, and loss of consciousness (whether through dissociation or literally passing out). During an anxiety (or panic) attack, you feel intense fear, maybe like your heart is going to burst through your chest. You may shake, have difficulty breathing, and feel nauseous, dizzy, or lightheaded. Anxiety can also manifest in sensations like numbness, chills, hot flashes, or tingling. Know that you are not crazy because you are feeling any of these symptoms or others. It only makes sense that your body would react to your abuse.

When I really began to look at the anxiety in my life, I began to realize my ability to reason and perception of what was happening had been severely compromised due to the abuse. I have spent so much time walking through life with fear and constant worry. I now know the toll my abuse has taken on my health. How could it not? My moods and anxiety reactions had been put on a roller coaster ride and I never knew when the ride would begin, stop, speed up, or slow down. I often wondered if I was having a heart attack, especially as I got older. Once I realized what I was experiencing, I was able to get to a place where I could walk through the anxiety while taking the steps I needed to calm myself down. I would take deep breaths, in and out, in and out, while acknowledging that I was having a panic attack and feeling intense anxiety. Exercise, reading, art, and gardening are all examples of healthy ways to quiet your mind. Again, you should always check physical symptoms with appropriate medical and psychological intervention.

AUTONOMY

n. freedom in one's will or actions, the government of self
An autonomous individual lives his or her life according to reasons and motives that are in his or her best interest and not the product of manipulative or distorted external forces. An

276

autonomous individual is not selfish, but understands that people cannot truly love another unless and until they love themselves. The beauty of autonomy is that *you* decide what is right for you and—if you have young children—what is in the best interest for their safety and healthy growth. As an adult, no one else has that power. It is your choice to be independent and your responsibility to take care of yourself.

BETRAYAL

Betrayal relates directly to secrets in more than one way. First is the betrayal of telling others' secrets, as I felt about my mother, especially toward the end of her life. Due to my love for my mother and not wanting to hurt her public persona, I kept her secrets. Every time I came close to telling, I'd become crippled by the damage I feared it would cause her. My feelings were not based in rational thought but out of fright. Secrets: what a deadly burden. The second way I refer to betrayal is the feelings of betraying the abuser(s). Being open about my abuse needed to happen for my own safety and sanity, and besides, they were the ones who inflicted the pain in the first place.

BLIND RAGE

Blind rage is referred to here in two forms. The first is your abusers. I believe everyone who has experienced abuse has been on the receiving end of a blind rage attack: an attack where your abuser's eyes go black and dark, blinding him or her to their physical situation and surroundings. This usually occurs behind closed doors without witnesses. These attacks are dangerous to the receiver and can escalate toward a violence and terror.

At the same time, however, being abused causes anger. I believe this is because we have been so stripped of our power, when our rage is ignited, we take the bait and it carries us away. Since I was unable to put my anger where it belonged, on my abusers, I learned that I would take it out on the people in my world: boyfriends, friends, and co-workers. I'd have an angry outburst and whoever was in front of me would feel its effect. I had also learned how to be angry from my family; they were who taught me to communicate.

Angry outbursts can cause us to spin out of control. In our emotional dissociation from physical reality, we can want to bring down everyone around us. Sometimes we are triggered out of nowhere and afterward don't know where we are and what had happened or why. Often, stuffing feelings inside and not calmly expressing them in an appropriate environment causes these frightening eruptions. When we are triggered, we must strive to allow ourselves to be *consciously* furious. Let the anger come up to the surface where it can be released, though non-violently. The anger we feel needs to be dealt with. *See: Anxiety, Getting angry with anger*

BOUNDARIES

When you think of boundaries, it is important to consider them in all senses. You must establish boundaries in relation to strangers and acquaintances, but in your intimate relationships as well. It is also important to consider establishing boundaries between your noise—your stinky thinking—and the purity of your true spirit and authentic thoughts. *See: Individuation, Separation*

CO-DEPENDENCY

I was a compliant child and adult, and spent most of my life in what I call my avoidant-holding pattern so I didn't disintegrate. Growing up in abuse caused me to compromise my own values and integrity to avoid being rejected by family members. With my mother, it was easier to put aside my own desires than to be sucked into her anxieties and fears, though in reality I was always entangled in that web, always seeking for my own happiness in the approval and satisfaction of others. I never was good enough for my mother, and therefore not good enough for myself. I was dependent on her to find out how I felt, so much that I never really knew how I was feeling.

All I wanted was the approval, acceptance, and love of my family, so did everything I could to get that. I was extremely loyal, putting more emphasis on their opinions of me than I did on my own thoughts and feelings. I was so bad at taking care of myself, yet excellent at taking care of family members by accepting, making excuses, and letting them get away with their behavior. I didn't know how to stop them, or believe I even could. All I knew how to do was come back for more. This, along with several other codependent issues, caused me to deny my own reality. When I asked them to stop, they didn't even notice. They could never hear my pleas. I felt unlovable and unworthy. It affected my quality of life on every level. My self-esteem was in the toilet and, whenever they felt like it, they would flush.

COMFORT IN THE DISCOMFORT

All my body knew how to do was react to and survive my abusive reality. All I knew how to do was live my life in turmoil. When I began my journey to change, I realized my unconscious mind and body thrived on the chaos. I didn't like it, but somehow I could be very dramatic—Academy Award-winning dramatic. Once I realized there was a life of comfort that had nothing to do with abuse, I knew I wanted that. Nice, calm, loving comfort. It was worth it, even if I had to work to give it to myself. I was able to shift my perception of discomfort from being "the norm" to something that would eventually kill me if I didn't alter its structure and my reactions. I confronted this consciously and behaviorally, one step at a time. I began to breathe deeply and quiet the internal chaos. Through understanding, I was able start replacing my reactions with nurturing thoughts said in a loving, kind voice. I focused on healing the chronic somatic reactions caused by my abusive normal. At times, the old comfort in the discomfort still appears. It wreaks havoc in my body both emotionally and physically. But as I grow, I understand why it happens and continue to nurture myself during times of discomfort, acknowledging its toxicity and challenging myself to steer away from it.

CRAZY-MAKING REALITY

The louder the critical noise in my head, the crazier I felt. I was constantly trying to fix the abusive situations and my ability to do so continually frustrated and beat me down. The message I received from my abusers was that the abuse was always my fault. I spent too many years believing this, and it became impossible to get a handle on it. My abusers were brilliant at twisting the truth of our reality, a tactic which, before I acquired my strength, always left me questioning my resolve.

How can we be constantly on edge, waiting to again hear how worthless and faulted we are, and not feel crazy? We are being manipulated—brainwashed by masters of cruelty, deception, and arrogance—to feel responsible for their behavior. How crazy is *that*? Abusers count on keeping you in this trap to maintain power and control. My abusers are the ones who are nuts, not me. I now know and believe this, though still have to remind myself during tough times. You should keep reminding yourself as well that you are not crazy—your abuse is.

DELIBERATE CHRONIC FORGETTING SYNDROME

I found, in my own abusive history, that those who abused had what I call deliberate chronic forgetting syndrome. When I confronted them about their behavior—most specifically their accusations and threats toward me—they never seemed to remember their words, would never show proof of the allegations, deny it happened, and never take responsibility. It drove me crazy. The stance of arrogance was always disgusting. *See: Crazy-Making Reality*

DENIAL

Denial is when we pretend to not see what is in front of us. It is a defense mechanism used when whatever is happening becomes too overwhelming to deal with. It shuts us down. To acknowledge and accept the pain becomes all but impossible because it cannot be coped with, so we pretend nothing occurred. The situation does not exist. It's a smart defense. It always helped me live in a world that made the abuse somehow tolerable. Making excuses for the acts and the behaviors of the perpetrators was the only way I could survive.

What abuse victim wouldn't want to live in denial? If we deny the destruction exists, it is not happening. If we live in a world where we don't feel, nothing hurts. However, living in denial keeps us stuck. As long as we live in denial, nothing will ever change. Being honest with yourself is extremely difficult when it comes wrapped in a package of abuse. You must get to a place of truth in order to take the steps out. Unfortunately, that entails feeling the real internal pain and accepting that it cannot engulf you. The cost—the pain—is low in relation to the benefit—a life of peace. Once you live consciously free from abuse, you can never go back.

DEPRESSION REACTION

Depression just makes sense as a reaction to how we are being treated, entailing feelings of hopelessness, helplessness, and unhappiness. Naturally, we feel depressed when our spirits and minds are being beaten down. If you are living in abuse and don't feel depressed, I would think there is something wrong with you, unless you are in denial, so numb you feel nothing, or use drugs and alcohol to escape feeling, as I did in my twenties and early thirties. I was trying to keep myself numb, but I know I was just masking my pain. Some find low doses of an anti-depressant helpful, especially in the early stages of their healing.

When we are depressed, we can feel unable to concentrate and quiet our critical internal voices. Our energy depletion may make us want to sleep all the time, but we may also experience insomnia. Our sadness is overwhelming, and we feel dispirited, dejected, and disheartened. We feel worthless and self-conscious, lonely and isolated. Our self-esteem hides from us. With stress so constant, we may think of ending our lives, whether or not we actually want to die. It becomes a deliberate practice to see the glass half full, and in this journey to find real happiness, it helps to surround oneself with the things that bring happiness. For me, it is my dog, my friends, the mountains, and writing this book. It has been working.

DISSOCIATIVE REACTION

When we dissociate, we literally split off to something simpler. We leave mentally and emotionally. The body is still physically present, but the mind is not, so—theoretically—*you* are not there. Many times, it is easier to leave abusive situations and mentally go somewhere else. This makes it difficult to pinpoint our emotions at any given moment. If you dissociate, come back and give yourself an encouraging hug. It is painful and scary to feel the reality of your situation, but you are strong and powerful enough to do this. Look at all you have survived already. It's time to face the situation head-on, because you know internally that if you truly allow yourself to feel the pain of the abuse, you will be left with no choice but to make drastic changes.

DONE

As in "finished." You'll see this word several times throughout this book. It appears in several chapters and references separate incidents. If you have been abused, you understand how elusive its meaning can be, and how it can be possible to be or feel "done" with something many different times. Being done with face-to-face verbal assaults may not mean being done with written or telephonic assaults. However, as long as we are caring for ourselves, we are leaving something behind. The goal is freedom, the truest "done" there is.

DOUBLE-BIND

A double bind is a form of communication in which we receive two or more messages that conflict with one another. For the receiver, it is a no-win situation where you have been set up to fail. A common way to refer to this is a Catch-22. No matter what you do, you lose. This is an abuser's ping-pong match. It's impossible for the receiver to confront the double message, thereby making it impossible to resolve the words. It is the intent of your abuser to keep you stuck in the crazy-making reality.

ESCAPISM

Escapism is creating diversions to avoid everyday reality. Escapism can take many forms: We may throw ourselves into our careers, grateful for the distraction but exhausted by the workload. Some travel with the intent of "getting-away" instead of exploring the world with curiosity. Others may form drug and alcohol addictions. Before I understood what I was doing, I thought it was better to be drugged up or drunk than to be in my reality. I was one of the lucky ones, because I made a horrible addict and hated how I felt when under the influence. When I realized what I was doing, I decided and was fortunately able to stop.

FAMILY

For me, looking at my generational family cycle of abuse helped me to understand the impact it was having on my life. As I journeyed forward towards freedom, I understood what I needed to let go of and how to let myself off the hook for it happening and for participating in the cycle. I have built a family around me of people who I choose to love and who choose to love me. The new chain starts here.

FAULT-FINDING

This was one of the many ways the cycle of abuse started for me. It made me feel insane because I could never understand why I was at fault, or why the abuser was making such cruel accusations. It was horrible to always be assigned the role of the failure. Another abusive method was to twist the reality of any situation so I became the one who was always wrong, belittled, and manipulated. My life had been spent navigating around land mines. Often, however, I couldn't wait for the detonations, so eager to get them over with. I heard over and over again, "It is all your fault," and "You made me do this." *See: Deliberate Chronic Forgetting Syndrome*

FIGHT-OR-FLIGHT

When we believe we are in danger and our survival is being threatened, our stress levels are triggered and our bodies automatically go into action. This hard-wired response comes from our brain, and, when stimulated, causes our nerve cells to fire chemicals which release into our bloodstreams and prepare our bodies to either defend ourselves or run away. When ignited in this way, the blood leaves our digestive tract and moves quickly to our muscles and limbs to prepare us for either outcome. In this physical and psychological state, our awareness and impulses sharpen as we *fight* for our lives and survival, or else *fly* to escape the danger. Our feelings of pain shrink as we become hyper-aware of our surroundings and situation to defend ourselves from the abusive situation we find ourselves in. It is our survival. It is a defense mechanism that affects our hearts, mind, spirit, and souls. And it does take a toll.

For me, this type of response had, and at times still can be, my constant companion. It kept me safe from attacks in the moment, whether psychological, physical, or sexual. The problem with this brilliant defense is that I took this response out in the world with me. I often went in to "attack mode" feeling the entire world was my enemy. What an unhealthy way to live.

FIXING

It doesn't work. Enough said.

HEART-MIND CONNECTION

My intellectual understanding of abuse was always good. As a clinical social worker, I understood what I needed to do for my clients and how to guide them in their journey. What was missing was my ability to do that for myself. It was difficult for me to access my heart due to the quagmire of confusion and the Crazy-Making Reality I always felt. In reaching health, I had to work hard on my heart-mind connection and merge what I knew and believed in my heart. I had to go in, get my little girl, jump in to the darkness, and swim to the light where I found peace.

IDEALIZATION

We idealize our situations to deal with turmoil and to attempt integration of all the impossible feelings we have about our abuse. We probably defend our abusers to the outside world, or make excuses for their poor behavior, but we may also defend our abusers to ourselves, convincing ourselves they are something they are not, or perhaps something they used to be.

For a long time I considered my father God-like, a saint. Every time he abandoned, I waited for him to come back to me. Even with all the evidence of how hurtful, irresponsible, callous, and painful his behavior was, I continued to idealize him and hold on so strongly to the belief that he loved me. I couldn't get angry with him and constantly made excuses, which did not go over well with the other members of my family. I held on so tightly to fantasies that he would come back and rescue me until I could finally hold on no longer and cut all ties with him.

My mother was known to the world as this wonderful and powerful woman. How could I go against that? I spent a lifetime making excuses for her behavior and pretending that her treating me in such a toxic manner was for my own good, though it killed my spirit and caused me unspeakable pain. *See: Rationalization*

INNER CHILD

My inner child has been the most important piece of my journey out of abuse. I had to learn how to connect with her and all her reactions to a life that had disempowered her at an early age. Exposure to abusive behavior affects children in many ways. For infants you may see agitation, disrupted sleeping habits, lack of attachment to parents/caretaker, problems with appetite, and general poor health. These infants may have the appearance of difficulty due to their perceptions that the world as unsafe.

As toddlers, you may see an increase in aggression (hitting, kicking, biting, etc.) because it is what they have learned, or is a way to get attention. They are trying to understand the violence in their own life and are working it out in the world. They may become extremely withdrawn and shy, or perhaps anxious, clingy, and fearful. They may get involved in the verbal and emotional battles because any attention is better than none. They may also show an increase in health problems like stomachaches or headaches, exhibit poor self-esteem and self-worth, or feel they can never do anything right. There may be increased troublemaking at home or in daycare, or the child may exhibit regressive behavior such as acting like an infant or incessant bedwetting after toilet-training. Of course, many of these behaviors can be normal. I am talking here about extreme reactions for this age group.

As children get older, you may see certain behaviors coming to the surface, some of which tend to be gender-specific. They may show escalated aggressive and disobedient behavior because that is how they are learning to solve problems. They may startle easily and have nightmares (a common PTS reaction). They may also begin to use alcohol and drugs at a young age to numb their pain. Overdosing is always a possibility. Symptoms of depression such as withdrawal, inability to focus, and a poor sense of self-esteem and self-worth may appear. There is a greater incidence of behaviors such as self-mutilation and eating disorders. Older children and young adults may be more likely to be sexually promiscuous or become targets for sexual perpetrators. In other words, these behaviors—regardless of age—may develop in response to feeling powerless in their out-of-control worlds.

(It's important to note here, as well, that not all who experience these difficulties come from abusive situations.)

When I finally felt I had accessed my inner child, I found her reactive and tenacious, but her constantly vigilant stance kept her stuck in a life that was scary and filled with darkness. I had to go in and get her, protect her, and let her know that I would not let abuse be our story anymore. I am building her trust and am in awe of her courage. The more I get to know her, the more I love her.

INNER TOWANDA

From the first time I saw the movie "Fried Green Tomatoes," I felt a connection to Kathy Bates' character, Evelyn, who adopts the alter ego "Towanda" from the story of Idgie and Ruth. Evelyn adopts the name and uses it in her quest to revitalize her life. When I need to infuse a little humor into my journey, I think of her.

INTUITION

The word "intuition" comes from the Latin word "intueri," which is translated to mean "to look inside" or "to contemplate." It is knowing something internally, a gut feeling, rather than having a conscious reason. It can describe thoughts and preferences that come to mind quickly and without much reflection, or provide beliefs we cannot necessarily justify. It has been a subject of study in both psychology and the supernatural.

My internal intelligence has always been strong, but for most of my life, I ignored the signals. I had to go in and start trusting its non-verbal communication, pay attention to it and listen to what it was telling me. I learned to trust my instinct and let it help carry me out of abuse. For me, intuition has been my most important internal guide. My problem is that I have too often ignored it. It has rarely been wrong, but, a small part of me still fights its wisdom. All of us living in abuse know on some level that it is wrong. Internal intelligence tells us so. Once I stopped ignoring my intuition, it has become my faithful guide and never led me astray when I listened. I ignored it and almost died in my bike accident. That will never happen again.

Listen to your intuition, for it is your friend.

INVISIBLE TEARS

Due to my stinky thinking and a rash decision I made in my twenties, I stopped crying. It seemed to make my family uncomfortable and increased my feelings of worthlessness each time I showed that emotion and was shut down. I thought I was being strong in stopping my tears, but I was wrong. For me, crying invisibly has created much inner turmoil. It is an ugly cry that weeps silently within, never shown to the outside world. At times the sobs are uncontrollable and stay stuck in my heart, spirit, and soul. No visible tears can be seen to the outside world and the sadness stays trapped within screaming for release. Now, as I search for this piece of my spirit and heart, I remind myself, "People cry not because they're weak. It's because they've been strong for too long." This old adage is my mantra.

"IT IS WHAT IT IS" AND "THAT'S ENOUGH FOR ME"

I use these sayings, well, because it is, and it *is*. Abuse was my reality, and by remembering these statements and understanding I could not change or stop the abuse, I could begin the journey towards health and letting go. *If this is what it is*, I thought, *I'm going to choose something else*. I know what I know: Being psychologically abused is wrong, and I am no longer willing to participate in it. That's enough for me.

LESS-THAN

The Universal Declaration of Human Rights (UDHR) was adopted by the United Nations in 1948. Its first article reads: "All human beings are born free and equal in dignity and rights. They are endowed with reason and conscience and should act toward one another in the spirit of brotherhood." Other articles in this powerful document include the right to life, liberty, and personal security, the freedom from degrading treatment or punishment, the right to the protection of the law against attacks upon one's honor or reputation, the right to freedom of opinion and expression, and to freely participate in the cultural life of one's community.

Mathematically speaking, $(<) \neq (=)$, so abuse counters our core human values. *And remember, no one can make you feel less-than without your permission.*

LIFE
See: autonomy, love.
Avoid: abuse.

LOVE
...shouldn't hurt.

ME AS THE COMMON DENOMINATOR

I was parentless during my life: a life filled with events out of my control, with psychological, physical, and sexual abuse as well as neglect and abandonment. Every time I tried to fix my situation, I would end up back in the same spot. Nothing ever changed until I realized that I was the common denominator in my own story. I finally began to understand the only one in my cycle and chain of abuse I could change was me. Every time an abusive situation would end, my participants would move on with their lives as if nothing happened, taking no responsibility for their behavior. I would be left stuck every time.

Realizing we are the common denominators in our life's journeys was probably the biggest ah-ha moment I ever had. We must take responsibility for ourselves and our choices to stay in abusive situations. Every time an incident of abuse occurs, there we are. Our abusers could be long gone, never understanding the impact of their actions, and we're the ones left to internally pick up the pieces. We are with ourselves wherever we go, and if we don't do something to stop our despair, we will live the rest of our lives in abuse.

MINIMIZATION

When telling secrets, it is not uncommon for outsiders to minimize the experiences of the abused. This happens for several reasons. The abuser(s) may be known differently to the outside world, or perhaps the person being confided in cannot comprehend the confusion of an abusive reality. Others may insist it is a "private issue," which is especially counterintuitive when help is being solicited.

NARCISSISM

Abusers fit all the criteria for being aggressive narcissists in one form or another. Their feelings of superiority and self-worth are grandiose. They are arrogant, cunning, and manipulative through their web of lies. They seduce with a glib, superficial charm. This goes against the explanation that abusers have low self-esteem and their goal is to pull you down to their level. What they portray to the world is their cover for their own insecurities and cowardice. The narcissism, I believe, comes primarily from their unwillingness or inability to look at their own actions and take responsibility for them, so invested in the need for their own self-importance. Without an observing ego, their abilities to self-reflect do not seem to exist.

When abusers attack, they show no remorse or feelings of guilt, just incredible self-justification and righteous indignation in their stance of superiority. Because their regard for the receiver of their behavior is non-existent, their actions are callous and cruel. They do not have empathy or the ability to understand or identify with someone else's feelings, and they fail to accept responsibility for their own actions. Their ability to internalize their behavior does not appear to exist. Bottom line: aggressive narcissism is all self-serving, and you are not even seen.

NEW NORMAL

Considering I didn't like the life I was living, it became necessary to create a new normal—a new life, if you will—and make a life that was defined by me, for me. How powerful is that?

NORMAL VS. EXTREME

In every relationship, there are moments of tension, fighting, and disagreement. That is normal, and healthy relationships focus on solving problems and finding the win-win. Love does not beat your spirit down in its name. When you are treated with derogatory words and actions, the only intent is to beat you down and keep you submissive. If you are in a situation where verbal and emotional cruelty is killing your spirit or the spirits of your children, you are being abused. Just because it is invisible does not mean it is not wrong. In the introduction, I ask many questions to help you define your own personal reality. Go back to these questions if you need.

NORMALIZING THE ABNORMAL

It is impossible to make sense of abuse. There is nothing normal about it. I had to dig deep to find and access the place within to confront the fact that I had spent a lifetime normalizing—by either minimizing or ignoring—the impact of abuse on my life. I had to strengthen my weak boundaries that had accepted this type of behavior. It required much vigilance, focus and constant consciousness.

OBSERVING EGO

Our egos, if healthy, are our ideas of our own self-importance. When they are constantly being beaten down, self-worth is replaced with feelings of insignificance. A healthy observing egos gives us the ability to step outside ourselves and take a look at what we're living, with us as the main players in our respective realities. It is a way to examine yourself, your behavior, and your situation. This is your ego observing your life.

An observing ego is essential to those of us who have lived and survived abuse to get away from our abusive situations. We must cultivate the ability to self-observe if we are to make the changes we need. The need for quiet reflection, really taking a look at your behavior and rewriting your internal life script, is necessary here. I no longer own the abuse. And when I have moments where my behavior is out of control and I inflict it on someone else, I am learning to acknowledge own my behavior and make amends. I am also better at recognizing the triggers from my past and

separating out what is an abusive reaction on my part. I will
continue to define what I want to put in place of the abuse and
the person I am working on becoming.

OBSESSIVE THOUGHT REACTION

You may have persistent thoughts that repeat in your mind,
perhaps with vivid images that are frightening and intrusive. You
repeatedly go over an abusive situation that has occurred trying to
make sense of it, change it, and fix it. This internal dialogue is
loud, unrelenting, and unforgiving. In reality, every scenario and
attempt to fix it fails. You don't realize the intrusive thoughts are
because you are living in fear and chaos. These reactions are
repetitive and irrational. They usually happen when unpredictable,
illogical behaviors are flung our way and we must try to somehow
make sense of them.

I had to first come to terms with the obsessive thoughts
existing and realize I *was* being affected. The noise was interfering
with my life on every level: emotionally, physically, socially,
professionally, and spiritually. I was trying to gain power and
control over the abuse in my life while remaining in the cycle. I
would become fixated and unable to let the thought intrusions
go. It was maddening, time consuming, and destructive. My
obsessive thoughts were constantly in conflict with my authentic
voice and would keep me up at night, then wake me up, then
follow me throughout my day, at times my week or month. It was
thunderous and explosive, and it wasted a lot of my time. It
followed me through most of my life and all it did was exhaust
and give me headaches. *See: Abuse turned inward, Stinky thinking*

POST-TRAUMATIC STRESS REACTION

Post-traumatic stress reactions (PTSR) develop because of the severe anxiety you constantly feel or felt. The psychological trauma forces you to come up with this type of hyper-vigilant defense system in order to survive your experience. You are constantly on guard, always expecting the next verbal, physical, or sexual attack and the emotional aftermath that follows.

These reactions can manifest in several ways: You feel intense fear and helplessness in your situation, especially at the time the abuse is being inflicted, but these notions of perceived threat can follow you around, as well. You may spend a lot of your time feeling agitated and disoriented, feelings about your trauma happening repeatedly. You are careful to remain numb and try to avoid another abusive attack and confrontation, or perhaps you create an abusive attack to get it over with. Your social, work, and family lives are probably severely affected, as abusive situations tend to beget poor or severed relationships with extended family members and friends. You may become more isolated and socially withdrawn than you prefer. Your personal safety and sanity is always being called into question, and you may be displaying self-destructive and impulsive behaviors. You may have problems both with sleeping and concentration, as well as stomachaches, headaches and other physical symptoms due to your abuse. You may feel constantly or frequently irritable or threatened and experience outbursts of anger. Your response to stimulus may be exaggerated and you startle easily. For example: the phone rings and you feel like you are going to jump out of your skin. I held my breath for most of my life. I still have to remind myself to breathe at times. *See: Anxiety*

PSYCHOLOGICAL ABUSE

Psychological abuse—which encompasses any kind of verbal, emotional, and mental abuse—is a deliberate pattern of behavior on the part of the abuser that is perpetuated systematically. It is always about the abuser having power and control over those they abuse, destabilizing them. It can be hard to tell when a behavior becomes unhealthy or even abusive. Being insulted, intimidated, humiliated, bossed around, or isolated are some signals that a relationship may be abusive. Checking another's e-mail or cell phone without permission can be abusive, as can jealousy or possessiveness, explosive tempers, making false accusations, or mood swings. Psychological abuse is everywhere, consistently being swept under the rug. This is why knowledge and understanding is so important. *See: Abuse, Normal vs. extreme*

QUAGMIRE OF CONFUSION

My quagmire was the reality of my life, my hole. It was filled with all that I could not comprehend or fix, what I was always trying to grasp and understand. It was loaded in a mass of confusion, living a life in the most confusing of circumstances. It was the events, the noise, the abuse coming at me from every angle. I could never escape it. It overwhelmed, took my breath away and never had a resolution. It came at me quick and effective, crushing me with its intent. In my quagmire were complex problems surrounded with impossibly out of control situations and unpredictable outcomes. It can still happen when I am hit with anger from other's that I am not prepared for which ignites my quagmire. It is a word for me that explains it all. *See: Vomitotus-too-muchus*

RATIONALIZATION

Rationalization is a way to distort the reality of abuse so you can survive your existence. This is something I did a lot: made excuses to myself for the behavior in my family. If I could rationalize their behavior, I could survive by convincing myself it wasn't so bad. Somehow, if I could justify their actions and the cruel, toxic words being flung at me, their behavior would make sense. This, of course, turns the abuse inward. I spent a lifetime rationalizing that which I now know was abuse. I made lots of excuses to outsiders about what was going on. I believe I rationalized their behavior because it unconsciously made it safe for me to be a member of my family. *See: Abuse turned inward, Idealization, Obsessive reaction*

REPRESSED MEMORY

Repressing a memory unconsciously blocks our experiences of abuse due to the intense and traumatic levels of stress produced. We simply don't want to remember. I often repressed memories that were too psychologically devastating to bear remembering. If I didn't repress them, I idealized or rationalized the events in order to survive abuse. In healing, I had to reframe the events in my life and come to a place where I understood they were not okay and stop accepting them. I had to bring the memories into my conscious thought and get honest about the impact of each before I could come to a place where I would no longer tolerate this type of behavior from anyone.

SEPARATION/INDIVIDUATION

Margaret Mahler (1897-1985) was a psychoanalyst who worked with disturbed young children. Her interest was to figure out how

298

these children find the *self* away from their mother or primary caretaker. If done properly, Mahler stated that the separation process should start around nine months old with periods where the child reengages with its caretaker to become stronger, separate out into the world and form an individual identity. She also believed that a disruption of this process could disturb one's ability to maintain a reliable sense of individual identity in adulthood.

SEPARATION

I talk about separation in terms of what you need to do for yourself to separate yourself from of the abusive relationship and individuate to your true, wonderful, authentic self. I believe that I reached a point where I didn't know where I began or ended due to being so enmeshed with my abusers. Their thoughts were becoming my thoughts. Their behavior was my responsibility and I caused the attacks. It was always my fault. As I became more conscious of my abuse, it became necessary for me to step away and separate myself from its clutches. *See: Boundaries*

INDIVIDUATION

As I journeyed towards a life away from abuse, I had to figure out who I was, my real and authentic self, without others in my cycle defining that for me. I had to individuate from the surrounding madness, establish my own rules and boundaries, and define the life I wanted. I had to separate out what was them and what was me. I had to catch up, grow up, and become my own person.

Though it is possible to individuate without separating, I would caution against it if you are able to leave your situation. Remaining in the abuse will make it more difficult to establish these boundaries and define your authentic self. However, every situation is different, and you are strong and intelligent enough to determine the best plan of action for you personally. Do, however, trust your intuition—*not* your stinky thinking, your internalized abuse.

SICK AND TIRED OF BEING SICK AND TIRED

This phrase is a big one for me. I had to get to this point in my journey in order to get out once and for all. Almost dying in my bicycle accident led me to there. I was through with the emotionality of my abusive environment debilitating my spirit and heart. I was just too tired to participate anymore. During this phase of my journey, I took a lot of naps. Then I'd get up, reboot, and continue working on building my new normal.

SHAME AND EMBARRASSMENT

...come from feeling alone, which you—we—are not.

SOMATIC REACTIONS (PHYSICAL REACTIONS)

Somatic reactions are a physical manifestation of one's emotional state. Notice how your body responds to abuse or to your triggers. During and after abusive episodes, I got chest pains, my heart would beat rapidly and wildly, and at times I would get sharp pains coming from my heart to my left shoulder, arm, and neck area. My breathing would become labored as my fists tightened. At times, I would go into full-blown panic attacks. As a child, when the stress would overwhelm, I would literally pass out cold. I've learned in recent years that I grind my teeth, tighten my jaw and because of this get severe pains in my head (TMJ).
See: PTSR

STANDS WITH FISTS

This phrase came out of a lifetime of standing with my hands curled into tight fists. Pictures exist of me as a child standing with fists on guard, just waiting for the next blow to come. I always felt pain in my hands due to keeping them so tightly closed. They were never used in violence or anger, but only for my protection. They are my statement of strength, courage, grit, tenacity, and— finally— empowerment.

STAY OUT OF THE NOISE'S WAY

The noise in my head used to debilitate me for hours, days, and— at times—weeks. As I began to understand it, as well as the noise of my mother and other abusers, I learned how to stay out of its way. You wouldn't stand in the path of a tornado or hurricane coming directly at you, would you? That's what I now do with the noise when its volume raises. I don't try to stop, control, or change it. I just don't give it any power. I ignore. I leave it alone. What started happening was the noise began to calm and not last as long when I left it alone. It now goes away much quicker by my simply staying out of its way. The noise is a learned behavior that was given to me; it is not mine. On those days when I have a difficult time quieting it, I don't beat myself up more; I'm learning to be kind, but still hate that I can waste time in it. *See: Abuse turned inward, Obsessive reaction, Stinky thinking*

STINKY THINKING

My stinky thinking came from my critical internal voice. It is what kept me stuck in those feelings of worthlessness and kept me stuck in my abusive circumstances. I wasn't good enough; I wasn't smart enough; if only I behaved better. These thoughts

301

swarmed in my head. It was the loud noise, my obsessive thoughts that repeated my abusers' cruel words, that was constantly in conflict with my desperately wanting to believe I was worthy of love and kindness. I fought with myself as much as I fought with my family, repeatedly going over encounters in my mind, trying to make sense out of my life and failing at the impossible task. *See: Abuse turn inward, Obsessive reaction, Stay out of the noise's way*

SURVIVOR

If you are alive and have lived in abuse, you are a survivor. You have overcome something inflicted upon you and come out on the other side. No matter where you are in your journey, know you are strong. *See: Victim*

TRIANGLE STRANGLE

One of the behaviors my father used ever since I was a young child is what I call the triangle strangle. It was his way of setting me up to compete for his love with all the other women in his life; and there were a lot of women, including my mother. I was in my thirties before I began to understand its ramifications. It was horrible for me and for all of the other women. I was overwhelmed with the thoughts of looking back at my life with him and seeing how he did this. Then I became furious with my father for having such little regard for me. I felt like a piece of meat playing my daddy game because of his damaged internal needs. For him it was *screw the women*, for me it was emotionally devastating. I couldn't believe I had been relegated to being just one of his women. I was his daughter. This was when I knew I had to walk away from him. This still causes me pain and probably always will, but it no longer controls me. Talk about a quagmire of confusion. Now I cry, though silently, for my father.

TRIGGERS

In working through my memories of abuse, I found many triggers I had to sort through and understand. Triggers are normal and you have them for a reason. They are there to warn you of danger. However, they do not help and only interfere with healing. Acknowledge your triggers, define them, and figure out a way to calm yourself down. The goal is to be able to gauge when your intuition is telling you legitimately to change your situation as opposed to when you are having an undue PTSR. Today I work on slowing myself down, quieting my internal confusion, and distinguishing what pulled which trigger, and what exactly happened when it fired. *See: Anxiety, Repressed memories*

UNACCEPTABLE

adj. 1. not acceptable, 2. what abuse is, always

VICTIM

This is one of my least favorite words. The day I described myself as a victim made me sick. This journey is about taking your power back and giving up your stance as a victim. It is about reclaiming your life with your rules, for you and defined by you. *See: Survivor*

VOMITOTUS-TOO-MUCHUS

My least favorite question is, "How do you feel?" It's the most difficult thing for me to articulate. At times when I tried to talk about my abuse, it would come out a fireball of verbal confusion.

It often made me feel like vomiting. It's a question that, if answered, would sound like: *I feel everything all squished together that makes it impossible to tell you how I am feeling. I feel too much all at once and if you ask me to tap into all those feelings, I will become overwhelmed, engulfed, disappear and die, or, if I show you, I will look like a raving lunatic.* This is what I feel when all my emotions come at me in force. Overwhelmed, I am unable to find the words to describe my emotions. I would check out, dissociate, simply unable to remain in my consciousness. *See: Dissociation*

WHAT ARE YOU SAYING GOODBYE TO?

When you step away from abuse, you need to acknowledge what you are saying goodbye to. In my situation, saying goodbye to abuse made me an orphan. As saddened as I was by this, I knew it was a better option than the anti-life I was leading. For you, it may be something different. Whatever the answer, it is one of the most important questions to ask. We *may* love the person and not the behavior, but remember: you do your abusers no favors by staying and enabling their abusive ways.

YOU AIN'T THE BOSS OF ME

I latched onto the saying, "You ain't the boss of me," one day when I was in a classroom of 3-to-5 year olds. As the teacher was guiding a child away from a conflict, the child whipped around, hand on her hips, and looked the teacher square in the eye as she informed, "You ain't the boss of me." *How perfect,* I thought to myself as I tried to hide my laughter. In that moment, that phrase became one of my mantras: "Abuse and family, you ain't the boss of me." Hold on to the goal of being the boss of you. It's powerful. It is hard work, but it can happen. You make it so.

THE ELEPHANT IN THE ROOM
Terry Kettering

There's an elephant in the room.
It is large and squatting,
So it is hard to get around it.
Yet we squeeze by with,
"How are you?" and, "I'm fine."
And a thousand other forms of trivial chatter

We talk about the weather.
We talk about work.
We talk about everything else
Except the elephant in the room.

There's an elephant in the room.
We all know it is there.
We are thinking about the elephant
As we talk together.

It is constantly on our minds.
For, you see, it is a very big elephant.
It has hurt us all.
But we do not talk about the elephant in the room.

Oh, please, say her name.
Oh, please, say "Barbara" again.
Oh, please. Let's talk about the elephant in the room.

For if we talk about her death,
Perhaps we can talk about her life?
Can I say "Barbara" to you and not have you look away?

305

For if I cannot, then you are leaving me
Alone…
In a room…
With an elephant.

WHERE TO FIND HELP

WHERE TO FIND HELP

If you or your children are experiencing any kind of danger in the moment, call 911 immediately. Make sure you have emergency money hidden for an escape. Have a hidden cell phone at easy access, or know where to find the nearest phone outside your home. If escape from the home is possible, run and run fast. Know the closest route to your nearest police station, or a neighbor you know will help.

If someone you know is in an abusive relationship—or if that someone is you—there are places you can turn for help. The following is a list of resources. The following referrals are for you, the reader. They are resources to begin your journey out of abuse, places that can help. I lead you towards them and have no personal stake or represent these referrals in any way. Each one is a separate entity that offers help. I cannot provide any guarantee that any of these entities will provide all the help that you need, but as of the time this book was printed, these are entities that have provided assistance for those living in abuse.Find the one that fits best for you.

You can contact me via email at Standswithfists333@yahoo.com.

ANONYMOUS HELPLINES

Child Abuse Hotline
800-25-ABUSE; (800-252-2873)
217-785-4020 - (for international calls only)

Department of Children and Family Services (DCFS) Info and
Assistance
(Advocacy Office)
800-232-3798
217-524-2029

Youth Hotline
800-232-3798

Missing Child Helpline
866-503-0184

National Domestic Violence Hotline:
1-800-799-SAFE (7233); TTY 1-800-787-3224; www.ndvh.org

National Resource Center on Domestic Violence:
800-537-2238

Childhelp National Child Abuse Hotline: (for kids and adults):
1-800-4-A-CHILD or 1-800-422-4453; TDD 1-800-2-A-CHILD;
www.childhelp.org

National Teen Dating Abuse Helpline:
1-866-331-9474; TTY 1-866-331-8453; www.loveisrespect.org

National Sexual Assault Hotline:
1-800-656-HOPE (4673); www.rainn.org

Girls and Boys Town National Hotline (for teens and parents; trained counselors):
1-800-448-3000; TDD 1-800-448-1833

National Center on Elder Abuse and Neglect Hotline:
1-800-677-1116; ncea.aoa.gov

National Suicide Prevention Hotline:
800-273-8255

Gay, Lesbian, Bisexual, Transgender National Help Center:
1-888-843-4546; www.glbtnationalhelpcenter.org

Rape Abuse and Incest National Hotline: (RAINN)
(800) 656-HOPE (4673); www.rainn.org

OTHER RESOURCES

Safe Place
www.safeplace.org; (512) 267-SAFE

Break the Cycle
www.breakthecycle.org

National Network to End Domestic Violence
(202) 543-5566; www.nnedv.org

Resource Center on Domestic Violence, Child Protection and Custody:
1-800-527-3223; www.ncjfcj.org

National Department on Mental Health:

1-888-793-4357

National Mental Health Association:
800-969-6642

National Organization for Victim Assistance:
800-879-6683

Prevent Child Abuse America:
800-244-5373

American Psychiatric Association (APA)
(703) 907-7300; www.healthyminds.org

National Coalition Against Domestic Violence
Phone: (202) 745-1211; Fax: (202) 745-0088
Phone: (303) 839-1852; Fax: (303) 831-9251
www.ncadv.org

The National Center for Victims of Crime
(202) 467-8700
www.ncvc.org

The Family Violence Prevention Fund
(415) 252-8900; FAX: (415) 252-8991; www.endabuse.org

National Resource Center on Domestic Violence
(800) 537-2238; FAX: (717) 545-9456; www.nrcdv.org

The Battered Women's Justice Project
TOLL-FREE: (800) 903-0111 ext. 3
Phone: (215) 351-0010; FAX: (215) 351-0779; www.bwjp.org

National Battered Women's Law Project
Phone: (212) 741-9480; FAX: (212) 741-6438

National Women's Health Information Center
(800) 994-9662; www.4women.gov

The Domestic Violence and Mental Health Policy Initiative
(312) 726-7020; www.dvmhpi.org

Health Resource Center on Domestic Violence
Phone: (800) 313-1310; FAX: (415) 252-8991

CPSIA information can be obtained at www.ICGtesting.com
Printed in the USA
LVOW10s0222271115

464309LV00001B/42/P